MW01005941

YOUR TIME IS NOW

# YOUR TIME IS NOW.

## Get What God Has Given You

# JONATHAN EVANS

BETHANYHOUSE

a division of Baker Publishing Group
Minneapolis, Minnesota

Published by Bethany House Publishers
11400 Hampshire Avenue South
Bloomington, Minnesota 55438
www.bethanyhouse.com

Bethany House Publishers is a division of
Baker Publishing Group, Grand Rapids, Michigan

Printed in the United States of America

Library of Congress Cataloging-in-Publication Data
Names: Evans, Jonathan, author.
Title: Your time is now : get what God has given you / Jonathan Evans.
Description: Minneapolis, Minnesota : Bethany House, a division of Baker Publishing Group, [2021]
Identifiers: LCCN 2020056513 | ISBN 9780764237119 (cloth) | ISBN 9781493431618 (ebook)
Subjects: LCSH: Self-actualization (Psychology)—Religious aspects—Christianity. | Christian life. | Joshua (Biblical figure)
Classification: LCC BV4598.2 .E93 2021 | DDC 248.4—dc23
LC record available at https://lccn.loc.gov/2020056513

Cover design by Dan Pitts

All emojis designed by OpenMoji – the open-source emoji and icon project. License: CC BY-SA 4.0

21  22  23  24  25  26  27        7  6  5  4  3  2  1

# CONTENTS

I would like to dedicate this book to my beautiful wife, Kanika Evans, and my five beautiful children: Kelsey, Jonathan II, Kamden, Kylar, and Jade Wynter. You are the motivation in my life for making every moment count. You are the motivation for my choosing to go forward in the call of God in my life right now. I love you all more than life itself. This is for you!

# CHAPTER 1

# NOW

**It's a word about timing.** A word that releases urgency when you say it or when it is said to you. You've heard it. You've said it. You know what it means. No more procrastinating. No more putting it off. No more waiting. No more messing around.

When someone says now, they mean *now*.

I heard that word at a time when I didn't want to. I had finally reached the highest point of my football career. After hours, weeks, and months of weights, drills, practices, scrimmages, and games for what seemed like an endless cycle of years, I had gotten the call. I had been signed. I had made it to the NFL.

To give you some background before we get going: I had always been the athlete in our family. For those of you who have listened to my dad, Tony Evans, preach, I was the child he would use in many illustrations involving sports. It could be football, basketball, or any other type of athletics. It didn't matter what it was because I had been involved in sports for what seemed like my whole life. My dad had plenty of stories to choose from.

I had started out wanting to be like Michael Jordan, similar to every young athlete growing up at that time. I loved basketball. But right when I entered high school, I transitioned to football. I played at Duncanville High School in Texas, and if you know anything about Texas, high school football is a big deal. Some of the high school stadiums in Texas compare with college stadiums in other states. Friday night lights are everything down here.

At first, I'll admit, I wasn't very good at football. I can't say I did much of anything significant on the field my whole freshman year. In my sophomore year, I did get a little bit better, but I still just played okay. My junior year is when I blossomed. I even started varsity that year. By the time my senior year came around, I had fully developed as a high school player. In fact, I was starting to get some looks. These looks came from Baylor, Texas Christian University, Oklahoma State, University of Oklahoma, and others. These schools kept an eye on me, which made me excited about going to the next level.

As the youngest in our family, I had watched all my siblings move forward toward their visions, whether it was on full scholarships for academics, singing, or something else. I knew I could follow suit with a full scholarship as well. And, as God would have it, He did use my talents as an athlete to get me into Baylor University on a Division 1 football scholarship.

If you are a Baylor fan, I need to point out that this was before Heisman-winning quarterback Robert Griffin III arrived, so we didn't win a lot of games while I was there. I like to say that we were laying the foundation for their greatness to come. But even though we didn't win a lot, I had a pretty good college career. In fact, it was good enough for me to get called up to the NFL. After graduating, I was signed in the 2005 draft by Bill Parcells and the Dallas Cowboys.

There were a lot of great names in the 2005 Dallas Cowboys draft class that you may recognize: DeMarcus Ware, Marion Barber, Marcus Spears, and Jay Ratliff were called out. I was thrilled to be chosen with these young players who had such dominant skills. I felt like I had made it. I had arrived and I was ready for all God had in store. Now was my time!

Little did I know, though, what God actually had in store.

To say that football had become my life by then is to understate it. Football was my go-to, the thing I loved most. My entire focus was football. One of the reasons was because for the first time in my life, I had to fend for myself. I had to fight for my role. My dad and my family carried no influence over whether or not I would remain on the team or even get to play. If I wanted to play, I had to prove myself to the coaches. The silver spoon I had enjoyed the benefit of for the majority of my life had been taken away. In a game like football, every man has to fight not only to get his job, but also to keep it. Whether it is your first game or your tenth year, every player in the NFL is in a constant battle to prove they deserve their spot.

Unfortunately, my first battle didn't last that long. Just two months after being signed, I heard the word that kicked off this chapter. I heard the word that signifies immediacy. Urgency. Movement. I heard . . . *Now*.

I heard it because I had been cut. The guy we all called "the grim reaper" stopped me from coming into the facility that morning. With his hand held out as on a Heisman Trophy, he told me I was no longer a part of the organization. I had to gather my things and go. No more hanging around. No more rubbing shoulders with the greats on "America's Team." No more reporting for duty. No more chances to prove myself. I had been released and needed to head out—*now*.

Words don't do justice to what I felt when I heard him that day. It was painful to be let go, to not make the cut and discover that you have been set to the side. To be marginalized in the one area where you feel you have what it takes is crushing. Football was my passion. But I had been sent packing.

What's worse, no one else came calling. I wound up watching the entire football season from home on my couch. I got to see all of the guys I had come into the organization with doing well on the field, while not being a part of it myself.

Up until that point, all of my thoughts and my entire schedule had revolved around football. Whether it was studying film or the playbook, practicing, choosing what I ate to best prepare my body to perform, or any number of other things, football was life. All of that changed when the grim reaper told me to head home. Years of a routine I had loved came screeching to a halt when he said, "Evans, it's time for you to go—*now.*"

*Now.*

The word can bring hope, or it can bring pain. It can make you smile, or it can make you sad. Whether it is attached to something positive or negative will determine how you respond, but one thing is for sure—you will react to this word. You will respond to this reality. This is because *now* involves timing. It involves movement. It sets the stage for something new to take place, and to take place right away. No more planning, analyzing, or choosing. *Now* means now. It's go time.

The Bible tells us about a man named Joshua who also heard this word *now.* He heard it at a time when both he and his entire nation were in a season of mourning. Their leader had just died, and their loss still felt like a fresh wound sliced across the fleshy tissue of their hearts. But God doesn't always wait until we feel we are ready to make His move. He doesn't always give us time to recover from life's bruises or knockdowns. He doesn't sit around until we give Him the green light. Trust me, I know this firsthand.

As I write this book, I think back over a daunting two years in my own life and that of my family. In such a short period of time, we have experienced tremendous personal pain through the deaths of so many loved ones, most of them unexpected. I lost my cousin, two uncles, my aunt, my grandfather, and my mom all within a short span of time. Yet while I was struggling to catch my breath under the weight of these compounding waves of grief, God didn't stop or let life pause. He kept putting things in front of me that I was to do for Him, for my family, my kids, our church, the national ministry, and more.

When God wants to do something immediately, He does it right then. He doesn't ask for our opinion or input on the decision. We see this same thing take place with Joshua. We read about it in Joshua 1:1–2 (emphasis added):

> Now it came about after the death of Moses the servant of the Lord, that the Lord spoke to Joshua the son of Nun, Moses' servant, saying, "Moses My servant is dead; now therefore arise, cross this Jordan, you and all this people, to the land which I am giving to them, to the sons of Israel."

The word *now* shows up in this passage twice. In fact, the book of Joshua begins with it. *Now* is a current word. It's a term about timing. Using the word *now* indicates to Joshua that even though so much change has already taken place, more is on the horizon.

The word *now* is also a reminder to Joshua that he can no longer ride the coattails of his mentor. He can no longer piggyback on Moses' relationship with God. After all, it had been Moses who had received the Ten Commandments. It was Moses who had talked to God as a friend. It had been Moses who glowed from God's presence while Joshua stood by looking on with the rest of the people in the tribes. Moses had been the man.

But as the book of Joshua begins, we are reminded right away that Moses is no longer around. He had done his part, and it was time for someone new. It was time for a change of strategy and an adjustment of plans. It was Joshua's turn to lead *now*. He was to have his own relationship with God as he moved to a whole new level of impact in his land.

## How You Respond Is Up to You

If you've read about Joshua at all, you know that he had spent his whole career up to that point playing behind Moses. He did so because that was the role he was asked to fulfill. If Moses told Joshua to go down as Moses went up, Joshua went down. If Moses told him to wait, he waited. If Moses told Joshua to fight in the valley, he fought in the valley. Moses was the servant of the Lord, while Joshua was the servant of Moses.

During that decades-long season of development, Moses had been the one who spoke to God, heard from God, and spoke from God. Everything revolved around Moses, while Joshua, at times, just carried Moses' stuff (Exodus 24:13).

But as we see in the first two verses of the book named after him, the time had come for Joshua to take on a whole new role. That's because Moses had died, and it was Joshua's turn to assume the mantle of leadership over the Israelites. He had put in his time, gotten the call, and made the cut. Now, everything was about to change for Joshua. Now was his time.

Much of the success or failure people experience in life is due to their ability or inability to respond when life changes as quickly as it did for Joshua. A person's capacity to adapt when necessary will determine his or her ability to achieve their goals in life. It shows up in a willingness to embrace the now moments in a way that propels you forward rather than remain stuck in a routine or role you have held for so long because you have gotten used to it.

The spiritual life is a life of development. It has valleys, mountains, and wilderness seasons. Like sports, it has changes in the coaching staff, equipment personnel, or even on the roster itself. But as we grow and develop, we reach that point along the way when God is calling each of us to a new level of engagement. This is the time when we can no longer ride the coattails of those who have gone before us. We can no longer rely solely on the testimonies of our mentors, parents, or influencers. This new season means it's time for you and me to have our own testimonies. Our own stories. Our own victories. Our own illustrations. This season requires our own ability to hear God's voice. It means no more procrastinating on passionately pursuing the thing that matters most—our connection to our Creator and the unleashing of His plan in our lives.

As you grow, it's not okay to sit on the sidelines of your faith while you watch other people take the field. Things may not look like you thought they would for you, but you still have a part to play and a role to fulfill. This is true even if it isn't the role you once thought you would be living out. Things may be different than you had imagined they would be. You might not be in the career field you got your degree in. Or married by the time you thought you'd be married. Or have kids. Or, as in my case, playing in the NFL.

But whether your life looks like you want it to or not, God has you where He has you for a reason. This is your season. Your time is now to get what God has given you by fulfilling the plans He has for you. The question is: Will you go get it? Or will you instead be content to keep sulking on the sofa, strategizing a way to go after that which will never satisfy at all? Or, rather, will you procrastinate on your relationship with God and the purposes He has for you while life's game clock continues to count down?

Before my wife and I started homeschooling our kids, my oldest daughter, Kelsey, didn't care much for the word *now*. She liked to procrastinate, especially on her schoolwork. She couldn't stand schoolwork. We would bring Kelsey home from school and tell her, "You need to do your homework now." But Kelsey wouldn't hear any of that. She wanted to go outside and hit the trampoline instead. She wanted to play, wrestle with her brothers, or do just about anything other than the work she had been called to do.

But our son, J2, was totally different. When we would bring J2 home from school, he would finish his entire week's homework packet on Monday. He would knuckle down and complete it all. J2 wasn't trying to see his homework again on Tuesday, Wednesday, Thursday, or Friday. He wanted it all done so he could be free for the rest of the week to do what he wanted to do.

Kelsey, on the other hand, would run herself ragged outside rather than do her homework right away. Finally, when she would come back in from playing and we would tell her she needed to do her homework before bed, she would complain that she was too tired, too miserable, and didn't feel like it. But all of her whining didn't change our minds. She still had to sit down and do her work at night. Why? Because we knew as her parents that she wasn't going to be graded on her playing. She was going to be graded on her work.

The problem many of us have today is this same issue of procrastinating on our spiritual work while running ourselves ragged in the culture, chasing money, friends, fame, or fun. Too many of us choose to delay our spiritual assignments while instead spending

When you stand before God, you aren't going to be graded on how you played the secular game of life. You aren't going to be graded on the things you ran yourself ragged pursuing for fun. When you stand before God, you will be graded on one thing and one thing only: your spiritual work. God will be evaluating whether you actually did what He created you to do.

all of our energy focused on cultural extracurricular activities that are not even on God's grading scale for our lives.

As you and I set out together in this book to explore your purpose and all that God has for you, I want to start off by helping you understand something very important. If you get this, it'll give you the foundation for everything else we look at:

When you stand before God, you aren't going to be graded on how you played the secular game of life. When you stand before God, you aren't going to be graded on the things you ran yourself ragged pursuing for fun. When you stand before God, you will be graded on one thing and one thing only: your spiritual work. God will be evaluating whether you actually did what He created you to do.

Now is the time for you to live out your purpose for God. Not when you're older. Not when you've settled down. Not when you feel like you've got nothing else to do. Ecclesiastes 12:1 says, "Remember also your Creator in the days of your youth, before the evil days come and the years draw near when you will say, 'I have no delight in them.'" In other words, don't put off what God has for you to do for another day. Don't delay it when you are vibrant and energetic to do the work right now. Now is your time. Now is your season.

Too many of us have become content watching everyone else pursue their passions and live out their purposes. We say we want to pursue our own, but we feel that it's safer to stay behind the screen and just watch others do it. We've become too afraid to try. Or too wounded from past pain. Too timid. Too cynical. Too stuck.

God knows this. That's why sometimes, as in the case of Joshua, something significant has to die in your life for you to come to an awareness that it's time for you to move. It was after the death of Moses that the Lord spoke to Joshua. It was after the removal of the person Joshua spent his whole life serving that he was able to hear from God.

So, that produces some questions:

- What in your life has to die in order for you to hear God's voice?
- What in your life needs to be laid to rest in order for you to have a greater experience of God?
- What is it that is keeping you from living out the full expression of your reason for being on this earth?
- What needs to be set aside in order for there to be a vacancy for God to step in?

As long as Moses was living, Joshua was listening to Moses. But after Moses died, Joshua heard from God himself.

I want to point out, of course, that Moses wasn't a bad thing in Joshua's life. His relationship with Joshua wasn't a negative one. When you read through the questions above, did you immediately think of what sin you needed to stop or what addiction you needed to overcome? Or did you think of a toxic relationship you needed to release? While those things may need to be addressed in your life, I also want you to realize that Moses wasn't bad. Moses was a great man. Moses led the Israelites out of bondage. The loss of Moses was a monumental loss for everyone.

Remember, it was Moses who carried the Ten Commandments down the mountain from God. He held up his rod to split open the Red Sea. Moses was solid. He was so solid and loved that the chapter right before the book of Joshua says the entire nation went into a period of monumental mourning over his death (Deuteronomy 34:8). They mourned for thirty days over Moses, although it was customary in Israel to mourn for only seven. They mourned for thirty days because the death of Moses was a big loss. But keep in mind, their monumental mourning was a precursor of a monumental calling. It wasn't until Joshua could let Moses go that he was able to live out the fullness of all he had been gifted to do.

Whenever you are going through a season in which you feel like you have lost something or someone you counted on, keep your eyes open through the tears. When it seems as though you've lost the one thing you felt you could hang your hat on—whether it's a person, occupation, health status, relationship, ministry, or anything else—be mindful while you're mourning. That is often the very time God wants to call your name because that is also when He can get your authentic attention.

It is frequently the good things in life that keep us dependent. If we are not careful, the good things can keep us stuck. They can keep us bound to what is good, unable to pursue what is best. God knows that for each of us to live out what He has called us to do, we need to be dependent on only one Source: Him. We must be independent of the need for notoriety, financial success, personal approval, family acceptance, or cultural clout—which is why a lot of times God will take those things from us and simply put them to rest. He does this so we will have no choice but to experience a vacancy in our lives where He can step in. Joshua got his calling when the only superhero Israel, and Joshua, had ever known was called home. Even though Moses was great and still vibrant at the end of his life, he would have prevented them from going where they were called to go.

There may be some great things in your own life—or even great people—that can't go where you are going. You may have to tell them, "Hey, I love you but I just can't take you with me." You must do this because where you are going they are just not called to go. You may have to step away from some situations, relationships, or even opportunities in order to step into God's plan for your life.

The Israelites didn't hear God's voice for themselves until they lost someone whose voice, to them, often rang louder than God's. Sometimes God will take things from you that you really love so you can hear from Him more clearly, even if the thing or person He takes from you was good. Moses was good, but it wasn't until Moses was gone that Joshua and the Israelites were able to go in and claim their Promised Land.

As we come to the close of this chapter, I want you to take a moment to think about that some more and just let it sink in. Do so by asking yourself a few questions:

- What good thing in my life needs to be put to rest in order for me to fully experience God?
- What blessing do I have that is actually taking me further away from the Blessor?
- Is there something, or someone, stopping me from hearing the voice of God?

Maybe there's something that is acting as a god in your heart that has to go. The Bible calls distractions like those *idols*. An idol is anything that superimposes its own importance over God's. Whenever you have something or someone taking God's position in your life, it blocks God from speaking to you (Exodus 20:3).

But beyond the idols that compete for our allegiance and attention, one of the even bigger challenges facing our Christian culture today are the men and women who have become comfortable just staying where they are. Had I become comfortable sitting on

God is calling you to go further, rise higher, and achieve more in His name than you could ever imagine. But you will never get to experience all that God has for you unless you are willing to rise up out of the depths of your own disappointments, get up off the couches of your own comfort zones, and pursue His plan for this season. Now. Not tomorrow. Not next year. No, the time is now. Your time is now.

the couch that entire season watching everyone else play football, I wouldn't be where I am today.

I didn't like the couch. I wanted to be on the field. But I knew if I were going to have any shot at something more than simply staring at a screen, I would have to learn to let go of the dream that had died so early on that season. I had to learn how to hear from God on what to do *now*. Too many of us fixate so much on what has died that we forget that God himself is still very much alive. And what's more, He has a great plan for each of us to live out (Jeremiah 29:11).

God is calling you to go further, rise higher, and achieve more in His name than you could ever imagine. But you will never get to experience all that God has for you unless you are willing to rise up out of the depths of your own disappointments, get up off the couches of your own comfort zones, and pursue His plan for this season. *Now*. Not tomorrow. Not next year. Not when your emotions have had a chance to heal or you've had a chance to try everything else out first. Not even when you feel more prepared, and ready. No, the time is now. Your time is *now*. It's up to you to get up and go get what God has given you.

Let's go . . . *NOW*.

## CHAPTER 2

**Just like *now*, this small word packs a big punch.** In just one short syllable the entire trajectory of a statement gets turned around. Things that appear as if they are headed one way reverse themselves with the interjection of this term.

We've been looking at my boy Joshua up until now. So far everything has been going his way. He got his commission. He made the cut. He was even named head-man-in-charge for leading the Israelites into the Promised Land. What's more, he handled it all like a beast.

After directing millions of people across a raging river, at flood season even, and on to safety, Joshua got them to march and shout around the walls of the well-defended city of Jericho. Doing so brought those massive walls crashing down.

Joshua had his own style and strategies, no doubt. He led differently than his predecessor Moses. Everyone saw that. They saw his swag. They also saw that his approach was working. He was winning. The Israelites were winning.

*But.*

The book of Joshua chapter 7 opens up with this one word: *But.* Like I said, it's a small word yet it means a lot. Because even though

Joshua and his warriors were whipping through their battles like wild men, things quickly went south. Joshua 7:1 tells us why:

> But the sons of Israel acted unfaithfully in regard to the things under the ban, for Achan, the son of Carmi, the son of Zabdi, the son of Zerah, from the tribe of Judah, took some of the things under the ban, therefore the anger of the LORD burned against the sons of Israel.

*But.* We read the word *but* because someone in Israel had decided to act a fool. As a result, everything pivoted on a dime not only for this certain someone, but for everyone else as well. In an instant.

- The reputation of the Israelites up until that point had been feared, *but.*
- Their army had toppled towns and destroyed its enemies, *but.*
- Joshua had become renowned as a leader, *but.*
- Joshua's maneuvering had proved near miraculous, *but.*

*But*, the sons of Israel acted unfaithfully and their winning streak came to a halt. Just like that. The victories they had come to expect were no longer within their grasp. All due to a man who had a change of heart.

## From Victory to Vanity

However, before we go and judge Achan and call him out for what he did, let's think about the Israelites' situation. God had been with them through all of their battles and victories up until that point. They had ridden the high road to fame and success. I imagine you know as well as I do what success can do. It can cause people to start smelling themselves. To start reading their own reviews. To start getting the big head. Which is exactly what happened to Achan, and the Israelites too.

We know it wasn't just Achan because the verse we just read says, "But the sons of Israel acted unfaithfully in regard to the things under the ban." Even though Achan would be the one to take the fall, he wasn't the only one who had been involved. No doubt he had help carrying his load of loot, with perhaps even a promised percentage for anyone who assisted. The Israelites had gone from riding the winds of God's favor to suffering the scourge of His anger. It happened quickly too.

Let's review:

- In chapter 1 of Joshua, the Israelites have a new leader. As a result, a fresh charge and energy sweep through the tribes.
- In chapter 2, they receive intel on their enemies through an unusual partnership two of them had with a prostitute named Rahab.
- In chapter 3, they cross the Jordan River on dry land, under Joshua's guidance from God.
- In chapter 4, they thank God and set up stones of remembrance.
- In chapter 5, they are so sold out to God that they are getting circumcised—meaning they are receiving the physical symbol that they are coming underneath the covenant of God.

And in chapter 6, they experience a great victory over Jericho.

By the time we reach chapter 7 in the book of Joshua, the Israelites are on a roll. They're experiencing the favor of God in their lives on a continual level like never before. But everything changes in chapter

7. A contrast is about to take place. A reversal in their circumstances. A block in their progress. All because some of their hearts caved in to selfishness in the midst of their success.

Keep in mind, not everyone went left on God. But as in any team sport or in military maneuvers, the actions of the few, or even the one, impact the many by default. Achan's decision to take what wasn't his altered everything.

## Keep Your Hands Off

Before we go further, I want to make sure we all understand just how big a deal this is. It may not seem like what happened when a guy took and hid some stuff thousands of years ago applies to you right now. But it does because the principle of his problem transcends time. Understanding it so that you don't fall victim to its trap as you pursue God's plan for you is a major move toward getting what God has given you.

This is because embedded in every victory you are given, and will be given, are things that are banned to you because they belong to God. If and when you start taking the things that belong to God, you can rest assured His anger will burn against you as well.

God told the Israelites to go and take the city of Jericho. The victory was theirs. But He also told them what wasn't theirs at all—the gold, silver, iron, and bronze (Joshua 6:17–19). God designated those things for himself.

Knowing how important this was and how tragic the consequences would be if anyone disobeyed Him, God even warned them to stay away from the spoils altogether. He didn't want them to get so close that proximity gave birth to coveting. He knows how one thing can lead to another in human hearts.

But despite the clear directions, Achan didn't listen. He didn't keep his distance. He wasn't okay with just receiving the victory and the favor of God. Instead, he got greedy and wanted to take the things that belonged to God, which were located inside of the victory itself. Achan laid hands on the loot and snatched what was never his to have.

This human tendency shows up a lot in Scripture where people set out to grab more than what God has given. In Genesis 2, we see it happen with Adam and Eve, who wanted more than every tree in the garden that they freely had. They wanted the one marked "off limits" too. For whatever reason, every other tree wasn't enough for them. As a result, Adam and Eve overstepped the boundaries God had given them and they paid the price. All of a sudden, contrast showed up. They went from enjoying freedom, provision, and victory to . . . *but*.

Adam and Eve had a perfect marriage in a perfect environment, *but* now they had dissension in their relationship. Adam and Eve had access to an abundance of food without having to lift a finger to make it happen, *but* now Adam had to toil in sweat to cultivate the ground. *But* they got kicked out of the garden. *But* Eve had pain in childbirth. *But* their son Cain killed their other son, Abel. The list goes on and on.

By the time you get to Genesis 6, God tells Noah to build a very big boat because God chose to reset the planet. He decided to restart this whole thing called the world. Why? Because mankind wasn't satisfied with receiving the victory God had given to them. They wanted more. They wanted to take what they had and add to it what they didn't, in order to go further than God said they could go.

It doesn't stop there, though. Take a look at David. In 2 Samuel 11:2–4, we read that he saw Bathsheba and took her, and the moment he did, he lost everything. I wish someone would have told David, "There are certain things that belong to God. There are also certain things that don't belong to you." But they didn't tell him, or if they did, David didn't listen.

God had already given David victory after victory. He had already made him first in line when he had once been last in line (1 Samuel 16). God had already given him victory over Goliath. He had given him victory when it was time for him to get away from Saul. David had been chased by battles but had continued to overcome. In fact, God had already given David victory over the Philistines.

But now David sat there one day with only one thing on his mind, and he couldn't control himself from pursuing her. He couldn't stay in the stewardship mode of receiving what God had given. David saw something—someone, in fact—that he wanted but couldn't have, so he chose to step out of line.

If someone would have just told David right then that doing so would turn him into a murderer, maybe he would have stopped before he started. If someone would have just told him that due to his decision he would soon lose a child, maybe he would have pushed pause. If someone would have told David that because of his selfishness, he would wind up with one of his sons killing another of his sons, maybe he would have looked away. Instead, he went after what wasn't his and wound up with family anarchy on his hands. His own son would later seek to kill him for the throne.

I guess no one told him, or if they did, David didn't listen. Instead, David set all of that and more in motion when he decided to take that which didn't belong to him, simply due to a lack of contentment with what God had already given.

Satan loves to run this scheme, probably because he knows how well it works. After all, he was the first to fall for it. Lucifer was the anointed cherub in Scripture. He was the second in command. Lucifer found himself sitting solid as the highest-ranking angel. He had already been given victory, power, and prestige. But based on Ezekiel 28 and Isaiah 14, he wanted more. He wanted to take God's position for himself.

But that was a banned position, since Lucifer isn't God. God is God. And rather than be content with a commanding role underneath God's rule, Lucifer wanted more. As a result, he wound up falling to the earth like lightning (Luke 10:18). He fell because he sought to take what was never his to have.

This concept shows up in the church age as well. We see it in the story of Ananias and Sapphira in Acts 5. They had been given victory. They were wealthy. Respected. The married couple had sold their land for a great price. But they kept some of the profit for themselves. They didn't give it all to God as they said they had. And because they didn't give it all to Him and lied about it, they lost their lives. Both of them died.

All of these contrasts, these *but*s, show up in the Bible because people didn't remain satisfied in the victory God had given them to steward. They wanted more. Yet as a result of wanting and taking more, they all got less.

As you move toward that place in life where you get what God has given you, I want to encourage you to remember the critical importance of this truth. As you begin to receive God's victories in your life, stay humble. Stay within the boundaries He has given you. Because once you shift from the mindset of a steward to that of an owner, you have overstepped the line.

Chapter after chapter, and story after story, this principle is highlighted for us in Scripture. If and when a person chooses to take something that belongs to God, even if it's something intangible like

If and when a person chooses to take something that belongs to God, even if it's something intangible like His glory, that person—and often those around them as well—winds up paying a very high price.

His glory, that person—and often those around them as well—winds up paying a very high price. So my questions to you as we continue this journey of purpose together are these:

- What things might you be taking that belong to God?
- In what ways are you seeking to act like an owner rather than a manager of what God's given you?

We saw in the last chapter that Jeremiah 29:11 tells us God has a good plan for us. It's a plan filled with both a future and a hope. God doesn't have bad plans up ahead. They are good ones. Plans to prosper you. But I hope you understand that He is the One who knows these plans for you. Because one of the worst things you can do is to go and take up your own plans instead. Especially when things start going well—when the money comes in, or the relationships get solid, or the career takes off. It's often easier to get off track in the good times than in the bad.

When we are experiencing victories in our businesses, victories in the expressions of our talents, or victories in our relationships, it's easy at times to think we accomplished this success by ourselves. It's easy to just help ourselves to the extra spoils of success rather than remember that everything belongs to God.

*But* . . . that's why Malachi 3:8 puts it this way, "Will a man rob God? Yet you are robbing Me! But you say, 'How have we robbed You?' In tithes and offerings." You can only rob God of something that is not yours to begin with. But Christians have been taking the plunders of victory by taking the tithe. That's just one way we act like Achan. *But.*

Another way is that we have taken what it means to be a kingdom man or a kingdom woman in marriage and changed it to fit our own perspective. Then we wonder what happened when conflict continually shows up in our homes. It's because we have taken our own ideas and implanted them into the victory of the marriage God has given us, turning it into a swift defeat. *But.*

This also applies to how we raise our children. I have five children, so I'm constantly learning, constantly studying, constantly seeking God's ways for me to lead my family. But one thing has stood out from the start and that is the reality that my children have been given to me and Kanika by God to raise, but they belong to Him. God said, "Let Us make man in Our image, according to Our likeness. . . ."

Our children are His. God didn't bless Kanika and me with children so that we could have look-alikes. He did it so that *He* would have look-alikes. It's our role to raise them to resemble Him. This is about God, not us.

Beyond marriage and family, our nation has also been taking and twisting the truths of God into its own version of reality. Multiple times the Bible says the anger of the Lord burned against the sons of Israel because of what their nation did. Any time you take that which isn't yours to take, you get God's wrath. Jeremiah 1:5 says, "Before I formed you in the womb I knew you, and before you were born I consecrated you; I have appointed you a prophet to the nations." God has given us the definition of life, which starts at conception. But we've been deciding for ourselves when life begins. We've been deciding for ourselves that we can abort destinies, destroy futures, and remove the imprint of God from growing within a womb just because we want to. We remove righteousness from our culture while wondering why chaos is ensuing all over our land.

Our culture has also taken the definition of justice and displaced it. We've marginalized it. We've stuck it on a dusty shelf out of sight as we skip over Psalm 89:14, which says, "Righteousness *and justice* are the foundation of Your throne; lovingkindness and truth go before You" (emphasis added).

Both righteousness and justice are the foundation of God's kingdom. What happens when you take half of a foundation out from under anything? Consider taking out half of a foundation underneath a skyscraper. What if you took out half of the foundation under the launch pad at the Kennedy Space Center? Or what if you removed half of the foundation under your own house? You get the point. Removing half of a foundation under anything will lead to its sudden destruction. Yet somehow in our culture and in our nation, we have decided that we can do that, and get away with it. But truth be told, we aren't getting away with it, as evidenced by the mess we are all in.

These are just a few examples, but the bottom line is whenever we take what belongs to God into our own hands, WE ARE ACHAN! That is, we are transforming our greatest victories into our greatest defeats.

## Hands Off What Is Not Yours

As you read in Joshua 7, we learn that due to Achan's sin, when the Israelites went up to fight the battle at Ai, they got beat big time. Three thousand of their men had gone up to battle but, in the end, they all fled. All but the thirty-six who were slaughtered (Joshua 7:4–5). The Israelites' defeat at Ai was so drastic that everyone reeled in its wake—"the hearts of the people melted and became as water" (v. 5). Even Joshua tore his clothes and fell to the ground, putting dust on his head. The elders of the land followed suit.

When Joshua had gathered himself enough to ask God why He had brought them out there only to humiliate them at the hands of their enemies, God gave him an insightful and quick reply:

> So the LORD said to Joshua, "Rise up! Why is it that you have fallen on your face? Israel has sinned, and they have also transgressed My covenant which I commanded them. And they have even taken some of the things under the ban and have both stolen and deceived. Moreover, they have also put *them* among their own things. Therefore the sons of Israel cannot stand before their enemies; they turn *their* backs before their enemies, for they have become accursed. I will not be with you anymore unless you destroy the things under the ban from your midst."
>
> vv. 10–12

God went on to tell him, in case he missed it the first time, "You cannot stand before your enemies until you have removed the things under the ban from your midst" (v. 13). The next morning Joshua and the leaders of the tribes went group by group through the families to find out who had taken that which belonged to God. It wasn't long before Achan acknowledged what he had done. He had stolen both silver and gold because he had, in his own words, "coveted them" (v. 21).

Remember, God was clear when He told them to not even go near the spoils so that they wouldn't covet them. That was Achan's first mistake. He got too close to that which was under the ban, and it lured him in. But after he got close, he made the decision to pick it up. He looked at it in his hands. He considered how he could hide it. He envisioned a future of luxury through this one easy move. Because of this, he arranged for a way to keep it rather than doing what he should have done right then: Put it down. Achan should have just set the stuff down and walked away.

Because he didn't, the Israelites lost a humiliating defeat at the first battle of Ai. And Achan, along with his entire family and all the animals he owned, lost their lives (v. 25).

As I am the chaplain of the Dallas Cowboys, I'm sure it comes as no surprise to you that I'm a Cowboys fan. Having been the chaplain for nearly a decade now, I'm all about the Cowboys when it comes to the NFL. When I accompany the team as the chaplain, no matter what city we're in, there's a red-carpet welcome laid out. America is full of Cowboys fans because this is Cowboys Nation. 😉

I understand that the Cowboys haven't dominated like they did in the '90s, but I believe we'll regroup and get it going one of these days! The '90s were the glory days here in Big D. The Cowboys ruled the land. Troy Aikman, Emmitt Smith, Michael Irvin, Nate Newton, Darren Woodson—so many greats. They won the Super Bowl in 1993, 1994, and again in 1996. They had victories time and time again.

Because of their legendary status in this part of the country, even to this day these men can pretty much get whatever they want whenever they want it. If Emmitt Smith were to call me right now and ask me to come tie his shoes, I'd probably head on over there to do it. "You don't have to say another word. I got you," I'd say before hanging up and driving his way. This is because these dudes are titans in Dallas. I mean, if Troy Aikman sneezed and needed someone to wipe his nose, he'd have a line of volunteers. These are our legends.

But you know something? As legendary as they may be, and as big-time as they are, and as many victories as they have achieved with their rings on their fingers and championship flags flying high—they cannot go into Jerry Jones' facility and take any of those trophies they won. Because even though they were a part of the winning

Super Bowl teams, the Lombardi trophies belong to Jerry and the Cowboys organization.

If Michael Irvin were to go in there and decide, "Hey, I'm a champion. I've gotten the victory. I executed the playbook and went up for the grabs when we needed it the most. I'm going to take that trophy home now," he would soon go from champion to convict. It would be a huge contrast that would come about immediately when he took something that didn't belong to him. Irvin's status would tumble—not because he didn't win in the past, but because he wrongfully took something in the present that would negatively affect his winning status in the future.

I hope you understand that Achan took something that wasn't his to have and because he did, he lost everything he ever had. He should have just set it back down. But what about you? In your own personal life, can I ask you to consider what you might be taking? Are there contrasts showing up in your wins and losses, letting you know that it's time to get back on track? In the moment of victory, Achan had chosen his feelings over his faith. He chose himself over God. Is it possible you are doing the same? I'm just asking.

The sad thing is, if Achan would have just waited a bit longer, he would have gotten even more of what God planned to give him. Case in point, in the second battle of Ai, God told Joshua that the spoils were theirs to keep. It says in Joshua 8:2, "You shall do to Ai and its king just as you did to Jericho and its king; you shall take only its spoil and its cattle as plunder for yourselves." But Achan didn't make it that far. God had the spoils planned for him to have all along, but Achan wasn't there to receive them when it was the right time. Achan missed out on all God had planned to give him because he jumped the gun in his greed and gave to himself. I want you to remember this statement: If Achan would have put it down in the moment, he would have picked up victory in the future.

Achan's lesson is a good one for all of us to learn and apply, ahead of time, as we pursue the maximization of our time. Let's not learn this one the hard way. It's not an easy lesson to internalize. Just ask Adam, Eve, Cain, Moses, Achan, David, Ananias, Sapphira, and so many others. In order to get what God has given you, you need to put down all that He has not.

Maybe it's a relationship not suited for where you are headed. Or a dream that is off-point from God's purpose for your life. It could be a mindset or a career choice. Maybe it's the way you handle your finances, or raise your kids, or approach your family, or . . . As God gives you victories in this life, remember to respect His boundary lines. That is, if you want to keep on winning.

The gold and silver Achan stole and hid in his tent weren't bad things in and of themselves. They just weren't his to have. What is it in your life, whether good or bad, that God may want you to put down? Could it be a dependence on people's approval, an ambition beyond His plans, or even a hunger for pleasure that prevents you from a healthy commitment toward personal growth and kingdom impact? Whatever it is, you're better off without it. Learn how to put it down. Learn how to stop complaining because you wish you had something someone else may have. Be content with what God has given you. Play your part in His plan. Go full speed with a heart of contentment, gratitude, and faithfulness based on what you've been given. When you do that, and when we all do that, we can all rise to win together.

You might remember the year 2020. You know, the year everyone felt would provide them clear 20/20 vision in their lives. The year we all anticipated, or so we thought. Have you ever reached up to give

What is it in your life, whether good or bad, that God may want you to put down? Could it be a dependence on people's approval, an ambition beyond His plans, or even a hunger for pleasure that prevents you from a healthy commitment toward personal growth and kingdom impact? Whatever it is, you're better off without it. Learn how to put it down. Be content with what God has given you.

a friend a high five and as soon as you go forward to slap their hand they move theirs at the last second and say, "Psych"? That friend was the year 2020, one of the biggest fake-outs of all time. It caused everything we had taken for granted as being wide open to suddenly close down. And so it was with the NFL. You know, when they started playing football games in multimillion dollar stadiums—without fans. I know I do. I had traveled with the Cowboys for several years as their chaplain, so much so that it became a normal, anticipated part of my schedule. But because stadiums were now closed to the majority of fans and staff, I found myself watching games on my couch at home . . . again.

I didn't get to attend those first games the Cowboys played on the road in empty or partially empty stadiums. But I talked with some of the players right after each game. As their chaplain, I wanted to be there for them to process what they were going through during this monumental shift in professional sports.

At first the players talked about how not having fans was such a big loss. They felt like they were going to lose the excitement and enthusiasm that comes from the stands. They didn't know how they would play at full speed when all the energy that once surrounded and motivated them was now gone. But after a few games, what the players began to tell me started to change. This is because once they got on the field, they realized that the loss of the fans around them actually forced them to focus inside. Losing the fans forced them to gain the internal competence they needed to win.

In fact, many told me that once they started playing the game and focusing on the game plan and plays called from the head coach, they realized that was all they needed. It was the loss of the fans that put them in a position to realize they didn't need to be dependent on what was outside of them. They had what they needed already, and it was enough. They had their shoulder pads. They had their helmets. They had their playbook. They had their calls. They had their skill sets. They had all that was required to execute a game with the goal to win, even if they didn't have the externals to rely on.

Unlike Achan, the players didn't mope at what they didn't have. Instead, they realized they had what they needed already built in.

I'll admit, I wondered if the lack of fans would affect the players, especially in the second game of the season when they found themselves down by a mile and a half. The cheer and encouragement from the fans often serves as a rallying cry to ignite a spark of hope in a team that has fallen behind. And after three fumbles in the span of just ten plays, my 'Boys looked dazed. If they could bounce back from a 20–0 deficit, it would be the second-biggest comeback in franchise history. Not only that, but they also needed to do it without a number of their star players who were sidelined due to injury.

*But.* My concern quickly was laid to rest. Because there in front of a near-quiet stadium filled with just over 20,000 now somber and disheartened fans, the 'Boys rose from within. My man Coop, Amari Cooper, started it off with a dazzling one-handed 58-yard catch. Then the team recovered an unbelievable onside kick. The Cowboys scored a total of forty points and snatched that win straight from the Falcons' mouth. They did it. They won.

All because they put down a dependency on people they really didn't need. They found the drive and will to win inside themselves and from each other as a team. They put down the reliance on external factors and external motivators to push them to greatness. As Zeke Elliott said in an interview after the game, "Look, they're not stopping us. We're only stopping ourselves; we're giving them the ball. If we take care of the ball we're going to have a chance to go win that thing."[1]

That's a truth bomb. Read it again. Because it's not always the enemy who defeats us as Christians. It's not always Satan who scatters us, as we see in the Israelites fleeing from Ai with their hearts melting like water. Too often in the defeats and losses of life, the root cause is our own choices. Our own wrong decisions. Our own impulsive greed. Our own covetous desires. Our own unhealthy choices in taking that which God has said not even to touch. Just like Achan did in setting up his people for defeat.

Look, the devil isn't always the one stopping you from getting what God has given you. Sometimes it's YOU stopping you. It's you giving up the offensive. It's you giving up God's favor, His victory, and His hand in your life. *But.* You can stop that cycle right now. You can change the trajectory of your life. If you will just decide to let go of the external influences and focus on the internal relationship with the Spirit and His rule over your heart and your mind instead, you'll move forward. You'll advance. You'll win.

*But* you've got to first put down those things you've grabbed that God has not given to you. In doing so, you will position yourself to pursue and receive all that He has. PUT. IT. DOWN! So that the conjunction in your life will be *and,* not . . . *BUT*!

# CHAPTER 3

# LOOK

**It matters.** Where you look matters a lot. Drive down the street and look behind you while you're doing it, and you won't get very far at all. Put your fork on your plate to grab a bite to eat while looking at the television or your phone and you'll probably come up with nothing. If a quarterback looks left while throwing right, the whole defense can get confused enough to miss the play. Where a person looks affects a lot.

Where God looks matters even more. When it came to Joshua, the Israelites, and the battles at Ai, God was looking at the heart. He wanted to see if the hearts of the Israelites were surrendered to Him. He didn't look at their muscles, their formations, or their skills. What God looked at was whether or not their hearts were in a position to obey Him. When He saw that Achan's was not, He allowed the entire battle to be lost.

But the Israelites didn't have only one battle against the city of Ai. They had two. The first one sent the Israelites running scared, as we saw in the previous chapter. But after the Israelites dealt with the mess Achan had created and got their hearts right with God, He sent them into battle again. Joshua and his men didn't just sit down and lick their wounds after their first loss. They got back up and took Ai by force. Joshua rounded up 30,000 of his best men and stormed the city, ambushing it and setting it on fire, hanging the king on a tree, then later throwing his body at the city gate to make his point (Joshua 8:1–29).

Joshua would go on to lead many more victories for the Israelites to experience as they came into their lives of promise. His book covers a season of roughly twenty years until we reach Joshua's death toward the end, by which time he is a man "advanced in years" (Joshua 23:1).

You might recognize this famous charge he gave before he left this earth:

> If it is disagreeable in your sight to serve the LORD, choose for yourselves today whom you will serve: whether the gods which your fathers served which were beyond the River, or the gods of the Amorites in whose land you are living; but as for me and my house, we will serve the LORD.
>
> Joshua 24:15

Those weren't just words. Joshua meant it. He didn't mess around when it came to his message. His household served God because he served God. Even those who came after Joshua served God simply because his legacy was locked in: "Israel served the LORD all the days of Joshua and all the days of the elders who survived Joshua, and had known all the deeds of the LORD which He had done for Israel" (Joshua 24:31). Undoubtedly, Joshua left his mark on those he left behind.

He had done things right and went out on top.

But maybe you're thinking right now that it's easy to leave as a legend when you were mentored by one. It's easy to rule an army when you learned under the greatest of all time. Why *wouldn't*

Joshua succeed if he had studied beneath and served Moses since he was in his teenage years? It's kind of like expecting a coach to win who learned under a winning coach. You expect him to know how to plan, prioritize, and make decisions. Or a player who played behind a beast: It's easier for him to go out and succeed when his time finally comes to hit the field.

Or maybe you are thinking the same about me. Why *wouldn't* I be leading others spiritually right now when Tony Evans is my dad? Of course I would be doing that because I learned under the best—a man with a doctorate in theology, author of more than a hundred books, and the first African-American to write a study Bible and full Bible commentary. Our family devotions were seminary-level stuff at times. And I hear you. I understand what you are thinking and I don't even fault you if that's what you're thinking right now. Because if I were in your shoes, and not mine, I might be thinking the same things. I probably would be. Because it would seem quite natural for a person raised and trained in an environment conducive to success to go out and succeed as well.

But what about those who didn't have Moses as a mentor or Tony Evans as a father day in and day out? What about those who come from a broken home and might not even know their daddy at all? It's hard to hold Joshua up as a target to someone who was never even handed a bow.

But that's why I love the Bible. It doesn't just give us stories of those who made it. Or those who went down in history as the greats. The Bible is full of stories for all of us, wherever we are on our journeys. So, if that's you and you're reading this book filled with thoughts like *This all sounds good, Jonathan, but I'm not a leader of an army and I wasn't born with a silver spoon in my mouth*, I've got good news for you right now.

We see this good news show up in one of the most surprising places. It's funny that when good news comes to town, no one cares about where it came from. People are just happy to have it around. So this chapter is for anyone who feels like an unlikely candidate for accomplishing great things for God.

We're introduced to another unlikely candidate in 1 Samuel 16:10–11:

> Thus, Jesse made seven of his sons pass before Samuel. But Samuel said to Jesse, "The LORD has not chosen these." And Samuel said to Jesse, "Are these all the children?" And he said, "There remains yet the youngest, and behold, he is tending the sheep." Then Samuel said to Jesse, "Send and bring him; for we will not sit down until he comes here."

The bottom line in this passage is that you have a picture of God telling Samuel that He needs him to choose a king other than Saul, who was making a mess of things. God told Samuel that He would show him which person was drafted to be the new king. We read the context for the choosing a few verses earlier.

> Now the LORD said to Samuel, "How long will you grieve over Saul, since I have rejected him from being king over Israel? Fill your horn with oil and go; I will send you to Jesse the Bethlehemite, for I have selected a king for Myself among his sons." But Samuel said, "How can I go? When Saul hears of it, he will kill me." And the LORD said, "Take a heifer with you and say, 'I have come to sacrifice to the LORD.' You shall invite Jesse to the sacrifice, and I will show you what you shall do; and you shall anoint for Me the one whom I designate to you." So Samuel did what the LORD said, and came to Bethlehem. And the elders of the city came trembling to meet him

and said, "Do you come in peace?" He said, "In peace; I have come to sacrifice to the LORD. Consecrate yourselves and come with me to the sacrifice." He also consecrated Jesse and his sons and invited them to the sacrifice.

vv. 1–5

So Samuel shows up, calls upon, and consecrates Jesse for the sacrifice and then says, "Hey, I'm here to choose a king." I'm sure Jesse was thrilled. I would be thrilled as well if someone told me that one of my kids would be the next king! But what Jesse does next should give us all pause. Because rather than call all of his kids to be presented before Samuel, he only brings seven. He leaves one out. You heard me: Jesse purposefully leaves one out.

It dawned on me as I was studying this passage that this omission didn't make any sense. Because if someone were to come to my house and offer one of my kids a $100 million max contract, you better believe I would not leave any one of my kids outside, and I'm sure you wouldn't either. Not when a max contract was on the table. If someone came to my door and said I want to give one of your kids this incredible thing, I would lose my mind. I would line them all up, whisper in their ears demanding perfect posture and behavior. I'd even bring my kids' friends over too and a couple pets just to make sure everyone was accounted for.

But Jesse didn't think like that. He didn't call all of his sons to the line. Which makes us ask the question: Why? Leaving a kid outside when a max contract is on the table could only mean one thing, if you think about it. And it's a pretty important thing, especially in light of how this story plays out.

I would like to suggest that there was something in Jesse's mind that made him feel like seven of his sons were likely to be chosen, but there was one who was certainly unlikely to even be considered. That's the one he left out.

Getting into Jesse's mind to understand why he would make this decision became my quest. I had to figure out why Jesse felt his youngest son didn't stand a chance. These questions took me to Psalm 51:5. It's a psalm actually written by the son who had been left out. It says, "Behold, I was brought forth in iniquity, and in sin my mother conceived me."

Now, you don't need a college degree to know what he just said. But if you still need help solving the mystery, this forgotten son also writes in Psalm 27:10, "For my father and my mother have forsaken me, but the LORD will take me up."

Surprisingly, this unlikely candidate is David. In my opinion, he has made it clear to us in these verses that he is a child conceived out of wedlock. He's what the Bible would consider illegitimate. What's more, Jesse knows God's strict standard when it comes to an illegitimate child entering the assembly of the Lord, let alone becoming the next king.

If we back up a bit to Deuteronomy 23:2, it says, "No one of illegitimate birth shall enter the assembly of the LORD; none of his *descendants*, even to the tenth generation, shall enter the assembly of the LORD."

If you knew what Jesse knew about both his youngest son, David, and also about God—would you have left him outside too? Based on this verse, David isn't qualified for the cut. Looks like David had a different mother than his brothers, and because of that, his family marginalized him. He was illegitimate. He was unlikely. He was ineligible. So Jesse left him out.

But God spoke through Samuel to let Jesse know it wasn't his call to make. After seeing all seven sons, Samuel told him that God had not chosen any of them (1 Samuel 16:10). Jesse may have thought he was bringing God all of the legitimate options to be king. But God made it clear to Jesse that the sons he brought as likely candidates did not include God's only candidate. The one Jesse had marginalized was actually the one God was choosing.

This reality lets us know something about God: He will often go to the back of the line to bring someone to the front of it. God will sometimes even overrule himself in order to dispense His grace in bringing the one who had been ostracized into a position to be utilized. God is not looking at you the way the world looks at you. God doesn't make His choices the way the world does. That's why no one is entitled to any excuses.

You can't say that your mama wasn't there or your daddy didn't have your back. You can't point to your family and blame them for all the issues in your life. Or say it's because your marriage fell apart and you're divorced now. Or even that you have a couple baby mamas, or you have children by more than one man. You may even have addiction problems or low self-esteem. But no one has too many issues in their life for God to select them. If that were the case, then David would have never been chosen as king.

David was chosen as king even though he was the most unlikely one to be chosen. This is because the God we serve takes people who are unlikely and makes them likely.

Let me tell you how this works in the Bible. Moses was a murderer with an anger problem. He also ran from his problems, hiding in Midian to avoid conflict. But God turned a murderer into a deliverer. Rahab was a harlot in Jericho. She sold her body to put food on the table. But when she chose to hide the spies who came to scout the land, God adopted her as His own. When you read the genealogy of Jesus in the New Testament, Rahab's name shows up. Even though

God does not call the qualified. He qualifies the called. When you understand that, you can never take yourself out of the equation. Your past doesn't dictate your future. Whether you were rejected by your father, were misused by someone else, or had a lifestyle that has been a wreck—none of this means you are not a likely candidate to be used by God.

she had a past as a prostitute, God saved her and used her for His greater glory.

Let's talk about Abraham. Abraham was a man who had a baby mama who wasn't his wife. He was married to Sarah but had a son from Hagar. Their son's name was Ishmael, who is the father of all Arab nations. Abraham's sin created a generational problem that millions of people still deal with today in the Arab-Israeli conflicts. However, Abraham is one of the greatest biblical draft picks of all time.

God uses the unlikely. He used Moses. Abraham. Rahab. David, the illegitimate one. God does not call the qualified. He qualifies the called. When you understand that, you can never take yourself out of the equation. Your past doesn't dictate your future. Whether you were rejected by your father, were misused by someone else, or had a lifestyle that has been a wreck—none of this means you are not a likely candidate to be used by God.

Far too many people have used their life circumstances as an excuse to walk away from the fact that God wants to use them for His glory. But please don't forget that in God's kingdom, the one who it cannot be is often the one who it is. Stop trying to disqualify yourself when God is calling your name. Focus instead on figuring out how God is going to use you.

I want to encourage you to never back away from your calling just because you have skeletons in your past. You think that you're unlikely to make God's kingdom cut? Based on the Bible, I say, that's perfect. Because the person who thinks it can't be them usually winds up being the one it is. Everybody in the Hebrews 11 Hall of Faith had a life of mistakes. But God looked deeper than what people see. He prepared them, called them, and used them for His greater good.

There was this man named Saul in the Bible who persecuted Christians like there was no tomorrow. He oversaw the stoning-to-death and imprisonment of followers of Jesus Christ. That was his mission in life. But God had a different plan. He met Saul on the Damascus Road and told him all about His plans. God then changed his name from Saul to Paul, and Paul went on to write thirteen books of the New Testament. God is a God who goes to the back of the line. He goes to those the world says are unlikely. He goes to those who were never even invited to the table. And He says, "You think you can't be used by Me? Well, think again, because I've got a max contract in My kingdom for you!"

It wasn't one of the sons Jesse thought it would be who God wanted. God wanted David. This is because God is riding a whole different wavelength as to how He chooses and whom He calls. Don't get twisted and don't be fooled by what you see. In spite of what you may have done or may be thinking, the God we serve supersedes it all. He gets to choose. And He's chosen you.

## Seeing What God Sees

Now, you might be wondering what qualified David if he had been so unqualified in man's eyes all along. What was the thing that made him stand out to God? We see what caught God's eye in 1 Samuel 16:6–7. This passage tells us what matters most to God.

> When they entered, he looked at Eliab and thought, "Surely the LORD's anointed is before Him." But the LORD said to Samuel, "Do not look at his appearance or at the height of his stature, because I have rejected him; for God sees not as man sees, for man looks at the outward appearance, but the LORD looks at the heart."

What qualified David was what God saw. It wasn't what people saw. David's older brother Eliab might have looked the part to most people. He was tall. Strong. He is described as having the stature of a king. No one would question God's choice of him. But God checked Samuel from the start. He didn't let him get too far down the path of those thoughts. This role wasn't about looks. Being a great king is all about the heart.

God had to remind His prophet Samuel that mankind sees the outer appearance but God looks at what is within. Stature doesn't hold a candle to a soul on fire for God, which is exactly what David had. We know this because Acts 13 tells us,

> After He had removed him, He raised up David to be their king, concerning whom He also testified and said, "I HAVE FOUND DAVID the son of Jesse, A MAN AFTER MY HEART, who will do all My will."
>
> v. 22

The seven brothers who stood in front of the prophet of God were the legitimate sons of Jesse. They were the ones who had been blessed with notoriety and opportunity. But something was missing. They didn't have the right heart. They were in the right place at the right time, sure. They even looked the part. But the qualification for worldly acceptance is different than the qualification for God's kingdom influencers. That qualification rests solely on whether or not you have the right heart—a heart like David's. His heart was like that of God himself.

It's become an obsession in our culture today to seek the world's approval—the world's likes—the world's acceptance. We go after it by trying to please people in what we say and what we post. But what's the point in amassing a huge number of followers who will

It's become an obsession in our culture today to seek the world's approval—the world's likes. We go after it by trying to please people in what we say and what we post. But what's the point in amassing a huge number of followers who will click twice to heart what you post if, at the same time, you are being scrolled past by God? What really matters at the end of the day? Or, better yet, Who really matters?

click twice to heart what you post if, at the same time, you are being scrolled past by God? What really matters at the end of the day? Or, better yet, Who really matters?

Your goal shouldn't be just to make it to the line inside the house when Samuel comes knocking. Your goal should be to hear God call your name. Because anyone can wind up in the house if you maneuver and move to the world's music. But not everyone can wind up as king, or as queen, stewarding all that God has for them to do. That takes a special person who has made it his or her ambition to connect so closely with God that their heart beats with His own.

I'll never forget a story that was told when the iPhone first came out. A man and his wife headed to the store to make their big purchase. They were excited. They had their fancy new phones in hand and couldn't wait to get home, plug them in, and turn them on. When the husband plugged in his phone, it quickly made the "bing" sound and lit up. But the wife's phone just stayed blank.

Here he was tripping over how excited he was to finally get to explore his phone but his wife's face told him he needed to help her, and help her now. "Babe, did you plug it in?" he asked her, even though he could see the cord connected to the wall.

"Yes, I plugged it in. The phone is a dud. It's not going to work," she replied.

"Well, let me make sure you plugged it in first before we head back to the store," he said, trying to tread lightly as he saw her response.

"I. Plugged. It. In," she said, again.

Even so, he went over to the outlet and gave it a little extra push, just to check. Sure enough—*bing*. Nothing was wrong with the phone at all. It just didn't work because the plug hadn't made it all the way into the source. See, it had the capacity to receive the power all along. But it didn't get any power because it wasn't all the way in.

We have a lot of people in our world today who act like they are close to God. They look like they are close to God. They dress like they are close to God. They talk like they are close to God. But when you look closely at the screen of their souls, nothing's there. It's blank. That's because they have not truly connected with the Source. They are in the vicinity, but just like being in the vicinity isn't good enough when it comes to connecting with electricity, neither is it good enough when it comes to connecting with God.

Man looks at the appearance. God looks at the heart. He looks at your connection to Him. The one whose heart beats in stride with His own is the one He calls out to do great things in His kingdom.

For me, having five young kids means I get to see all the new kids movies that come to the theater. Yes, *get* to see, because most of those movies are pretty good! Especially *The Lion King*. I hope you went and saw it, or rented it. It's an age-old story in which the young lion, Simba, is trained by his father. But when Simba goes to a place he isn't supposed to go, his dad, Mufasa, has to go after him to save him. Yet in the process of his dad saving him, as the story goes, his dad died.

Then, to make matters worse, his uncle Scar lies to Simba and tells him it's all his fault. He makes the young lion fearful. He makes him feel down. He makes him feel illegitimate. All of these emotions racing around in Simba cause him to run away. He questions his own abilities and starts hanging around others who are content to simply wander with him.

That is, until the day that the one who died, his father, appears in a cloud to remind him that he was not put on this earth to wander around and eat grubs. He reminds him that he is a king, destined to rule and guide others to safety.

Because Simba listened to the wise words of his father, he has the courage to face "the Scar" that sought to exclude him from his rightful place on the throne. He faces the pain of the past and chooses to conquer it rather than be bound by it. As a result, he claims his calling on Pride Rock, leading those he was created to lead.

We also have a Savior who died and came back to life. He's here to let each of us know that we are called to a higher purpose than our past may suggest. He wants us to know that we are never to allow the scars or situations of life to cause us to think less of ourselves. God has called us to the top of the mountain in order to love and lead according to His principles and purposes.

Some of us think we're waiting on God to tell us that our time is now. But God is waiting on you to seize it. He's already done the work. He's already called you. He's already chosen you. He's waiting for you to take your rightful place by facing your scars and leaving them behind. They can only hold you back if you let them.

Ephesians 1:3 tells us that we have all we need right now to be all we can be for Christ. It says, "Blessed be the God and Father of our Lord Jesus Christ, who has blessed us with every spiritual blessing in the heavenly places in Christ." The words "who has blessed" are past tense. The blessings are already yours. The favor is already yours. The time is already yours, right now. It's up to you to realize your value and your position and start walking in it. Your scars no longer own you. See what God sees . . . *LOOK*.

## Scan to Watch

 You will see a movie on getting what God has given you. Look for codes at the end of chapters 6 and 9 as well.

# CHAPTER 4

**It's a big word in a small package.** Without it, we're stuck. With it, everything is on the table. This word *go* changes everything. You can study what *go* means in any of the languages you want, but what you'll find out by the time you're done is that *go* means just that: *Go*. It literally renders, "to move on a course: PROCEED."[1] In other words, *go*.

Yet even though so many of us know what this little word means, we remain stuck where we are. That's because while *go* is an easy word to interpret, it's a challenging word to live out. We'll see more of the reason why as we look at the life of Abraham in a bit. But first, I want to prepare our hearts for these principles through the story of a little girl who was trying to earn some money so she could go to the candy store. She was working hard at home doing the chores her parents gave her in order to earn her allowance. Finally, she earned two dollars. When it came time for her to go to the candy store with her dad, she was ready. She knew what she wanted to pick out. She felt pride in her hard work and anticipated her reward.

The problem came when she got out of the car with her dad. He asked her to hold his hand as they walked across the parking lot so she wouldn't get hurt. But the hand she used to grasp her dad's was the same hand she was using to hold her two dollars. Before she knew it, the wind blew away everything she had worked so hard to earn.

The little girl instantly tried to let go of her dad's hand to go and chase her money but her daddy wouldn't loosen his grip. He didn't allow her to chase after her money. The money blew out to the road where the cars were driving, and he explained to her that she would get hurt if she set out after it.

Tears came to her eyes as she tried to pry her hand loose, but she knew her dad would never let go, so she eventually gave up. But she also noticed he had kept walking toward the candy store, even though she no longer had any money to buy what she wanted. As they walked through the door of the candy store, she saw her dad reach into his pocket and pull out a twenty dollar bill. In that moment she realized that being with her father was much more valuable than chasing after what she had worked for and lost.

Many of us have worked hard to achieve the expectations we have for our own lives. We have pursued our own plans. We've set up our own goals, markers, savings, and hopes. But this story reminds me, and should remind each of us, that what God has in His pocket is exceedingly and abundantly more than we ever even dreamed of (Ephesians 3:20). He has called us to a journey of greatness. It's a pathway to purpose. It's a plan to accomplish more for His kingdom than we ever could accomplish on our own.

Nowhere do I see this plan laid out for us more clearly in Scripture than it is in Genesis 12. This passage gives us a glimpse into a great promise God has made to Abraham (then named Abram). These verses contain the blueprint for a man who held God's hand all the way to the end zone of life. It's one of my favorite passages

There is always a journey to every victory in life. It's not just about getting to the promises. Often, it's the path along the way that shapes you, molds you, and makes you into the greatness you seek. If you don't participate and cooperate with the journey itself, how is God going to unleash it? No athlete just shows up ready to play. There is always a journey toward greatness.

of Scripture because it gives us insight into how we can get all that God has in store for us as well. The first three verses set the scene:

Now the LORD said to Abram,

> "Go forth from your country,
> And from your relatives
> And from your father's house,
> To the land which I will show you;
> And I will make you a great nation,
> And I will bless you,
> And make your name great;
> And so you shall be a blessing;
> And I will bless those who bless you,
> And the one who curses you I will curse.
> And in you all the families of the earth will be blessed."

That sounds like a great promise, doesn't it? That sounds like a bright future in addition to a lasting legacy. As a reminder, we are all Abraham's children as followers of Christ. Galatians 3:29 explains, "And if you belong to Christ, then you are Abraham's descendants, heirs according to promise." In Christ, you are an heir to Abraham and his promises. In Christ, I am an heir to Abraham and his promises. In short, God would not have put us here if He did not have something in store for our lives.

God's got a plan for you based on His kingdom and His agenda. Greatness sits on the precipice of your life waiting for you to reach out and grab it. But first, there is a journey you must undertake that has everything to do with when you will reach this greatness.

There is always a journey to every victory in life. It's not just about getting to the promises. Often, it's the path along the way that shapes you, molds you, and makes you into the greatness you seek. If you don't participate and cooperate with the journey itself, how is God going to unleash it? No athlete just shows up ready to play. There is always a journey toward greatness. No musician just shows up ready to master his or her instrument. There is always a journey toward greatness.

Greatness is a process. There are many people who have not achieved the promises God has for them because they got too caught up in chasing their own expectations and failed to focus on God's journey for them. God told Abraham to travel from his homeland—his family—and his father's house to the land God would show him before revealing the full extent of His great plan for him. He told him to get in the gym, or the practice room, and get to work first.

The problem we see when we come upon this passage in Genesis 12 and Abraham's call to get up and go, though, is that Abraham had settled down by then. He was in a position where most people feel like they have already made it. Genesis 11:31 tells us,

> Terah took Abram his son, and Lot the son of Haran, his grandson, and Sarai his daughter-in-law, his son Abram's wife; and they went out together from Ur of the Chaldeans in order to enter the land of Canaan; and they went as far as Haran, and settled there.

To go "as far as" implies that there was still further to go. But regardless of that truth, they had chosen to settle. Settled is different than camped. Camped means you're still planning to continue traveling. You're just taking a break. Camping is like a rest station, not a permanent space. But Abraham hadn't just camped. Abraham had settled. He had dropped anchor. Stopped. Finished. He was good where he was.

But God wasn't. God wasn't good with Abraham having gone only "as far as" but not all the way into the Promised Land. That's why the word of the Lord came to Abraham, to unsettle him from the place he had settled.

That tells me something. When God's Word comes to you, it is not always to just settle you in your own thoughts. He is coming to you—and to me—to unsettle those who are settled. His plan for you and your plan for you are often in two different locations. And just because you are settled, have met your personal goals, and have reached the expectations you have for your life, career, finances, and family doesn't mean God is okay with it. It doesn't mean God is finished with you yet. He knows where He plans to take you and maximize you for His purposes.

Most of us approach God's Word all wrong. Most of us go to God's Word and assume that He is telling us what we are already thinking. Most of us go to the Bible to rubber-stamp our own thoughts. And we'll just keep flipping through the pages until we find the verse that justifies our own decisions. But that's not how God works. When God speaks, He is frequently speaking to unsettle those who are settled.

He speaks to get you to think differently than your normal train of thought. You know when God is really speaking to you because your response is more along the lines of "C'mon, Jesus, stop. I'm fine where I am." You're trying to get Him off of you because you've already settled on a location, a path, and a plan. You've already put down roots in your way of operating. You've settled in your place. But what God is saying—more often than not—is that He is not finished. It's not the end of the game. It may have been a good play or a good score. It might even have been a good series. But the game is still going, and you've got more to do.

Far too often many of us get stuck thinking that when our plans and expectations have been met, God's plans and expectations have been met too. But just as God said to Abraham, He has a destiny out there for you. God doesn't exist to be a reinforcement to your own omniscience. That's not why He's here. Isaiah 55:8–9 says,

> "For My thoughts are not your thoughts,
> Nor are your ways My ways," declares the LORD.
> "For as the heavens are higher than the earth,
> So are My ways higher than your ways
> And My thoughts than your thoughts."

God is not here to reinforce your thoughts or to help you follow your deceitful heart (Jeremiah 17:9). He's here to unsettle you. He's changing the game plan.

When you look at characters in the Bible and how God used them, He always changed their plans. Sarah was old enough to be a grandmother by the time she got pregnant with her son of the promise. Noah had no ambition to be a boat builder in a world without rain. David wasn't daydreaming of becoming a king as he watched over the sheep. None of these individuals had thoughts set on where God was taking them. This is because God was taking them to a totally different place. He was not merging His thoughts with theirs. He was sticking to His own because His path contained the promise of true greatness.

The plan I had for my life—that of playing in the NFL for ten years, then settling down and having a family, wasn't the plan God had for me. I had it all scoped out in my mind: I'd play as a fullback for ten years. I'd save all my money. Then I'd get married, go buy a house in a tropical location, simulcast some teachings with my dad while sitting on a beach and experiencing the luxuries of life. I had already dreamed all of this up when God grabbed ahold of my arm and said, "Stay here with Me."

Now, God knows how many years I wasted reaching back for my own dreams while He kept holding firmly to my hand saying, "Jonathan, stay here with Me. My plan is better than all of that. You just can't see it yet." And we do that, don't we? We postpone our own God-given promises by reaching back for what was never ours.

Many of you may be on a similar journey, tugging on the hand of God trying to free yourself rather than surrendering to His lead in your life. You're looking at what you've lost and you're still trying to come up with ways to get it. You're scheming. You're strategizing. You're trying to work it out. But God is holding you firmly, saying, "Stay here with Me."

Or it might be you feel like you've finally reached that place where all your bills get paid, you get enough free time to make work worth it, and you don't want to rock the boat. But God is saying, "Go here with Me." He's pulling you in a direction away from the space you are in now that is so comfortable. You are settled. You don't want to grind anymore.

Abraham was old and settled by the time God told him to get up and head over to Canaan. Canaan wasn't comfortable. Canaan was full of enemies, dangers, and the great unknown. The unknown, on its own, is enough to keep most of us planted firmly where we are.

But when God calls you, expect the unexpected. Know there will be unknowns. God's calling is never to settle you. Rather, it is often to rip you from your comfort zone so you no longer depend on yourself, your skills, and your own understanding. God told Abraham, in short: Leave your country. Leave your relatives. Leave your father's house. Leave what you know. Leave the comfort. Leave the couch. *Go.*

God doesn't mind waiting to deliver your promise until you prove yourself trustworthy in following Him during these times of testing. He wants to make sure you are ready for the promise when you reach it. He wants to make sure you are mature enough to handle it when it's your time to have it. He wants to make sure you are positioned to retain it and manage it well, and that you won't blow it.

I remember when I played in the NFL under Coach Bill Parcells. One of the first things he did when we came to training camp was adjust our stance. The stance for a football player is the starting point. It's how you get ready before you go. But Coach wanted to fiddle with it. He wanted to address it, even though my stance was a position I had gone to for more than eight years by then. He didn't care. He didn't want us to rely on what had gotten us to that point. Because what had gotten us to that point may have worked in college and in high school, but this new level wasn't either of those. The plays were different in the NFL. The players were different too. This was a whole other level and our stance needed to reflect that.

For some of us in our Christian walk, we need to change our stance. We need to change how we roll. We need to address how we make our decisions, talk to our spouse, or relate to our friends and family. We need to change our stance on how we serve in the church. We need to change our stance on how we deal with our money. We need to change our stance on how we spend time with God, in His Word, or aligning our thoughts under His. We need to change our stance in all of these areas because this is our shot in a whole new league—it's called the Kingdom of God.

The spiritual warfare is different than the physical troubles we have known for so long. The warriors we battle are different. The weapons are different. The approach is different. In order to make it in this spiritual league, you've got to be willing to let go and leave all that you know if it is preventing you from experiencing the journey of greatness God has called you to live out. You may need to

- Leave your thoughts behind.
- Leave your will at the door.
- Leave your history.
- Leave your hopes.
- Leave your perspective and your patterns.

Adjust your stance. Sometimes you have to leave the things you think you need in order to get the greatness you know you want. If it goes against what God says, leave it. Drop it. Walk away. Like Achan should have done as we saw in an earlier chapter, just put it down. Because anything that disagrees with biblical truth needs to go in order for you to get up, go, and get what God has given you.

When you feel the Spirit prodding you to do something different, to be different, to go to a different place—and you're uncomfortable with it—that's a sign that you need to pack your bags and go. If you start to feel comfortable in a shackled situation, that's a dangerous place to be. You'll never get all that God has for you if you stay stuck to what you know.

Too many of us want assurance from God that the grass on the other side of the fence is as green as that which we are standing on right now, or greener. But the truth is that you must go before God will show. Yes, it's an uncomfortable feeling. Yes, it's a stretching experience. No, there are no guarantees. But isn't that what faith is all about? Faith is being sure of what you can't see, not what you can. There are not those kinds of guarantees in faith, or it wouldn't be faith.

Ask yourself what thing or place or direction is your *go*. What have you been fighting, resisting, and maneuvering your way out of for years? Remember: When you go, God will show. He will pull your unique promise out of His pocket.

## What's the Secret?

Before we go deeper, I want you to take a moment to think. Ask yourself what thing or place or direction is your *go*. What have you been fighting, resisting, and maneuvering your way out of for years? Remember: When you go, God will show. He will pull your unique promise out of His pocket. And the moment He does you will realize that being with the Father is more valuable than anything else you were chasing or trying to hold on to.

I remember a day I sat down with my dad when I was in the twelfth grade because I wanted to know how he had made it from Point A to Point B in his life. I had to figure it out because in my life, I had reached a stage of pseudo-maturity where I decided that I didn't want to mess up this thing called life. I wanted to know how to make my first attempt at "getting it right" my best attempt. So I asked my dad how he had overcome major obstacles in is life: being raised by a father who was a high school dropout and a mother who for a long time was far from God. Growing up in the rough inner city of Baltimore that gives rise to some of our nation's worst statistics. How in the world did he make it out? I needed to know. I wanted to learn lessons from his journey to greatness. So I asked him to tell me how.

He asked me, "Son, do you really want to know?"

I bantered, "Yeah, Dad, I really want to know. That's why I'm sitting here looking at you!"

He said, "Jon Jon, go read Hebrews 11 and tell me what you see."

I shrugged my shoulders and rolled my eyes as a sign of my disappointment in his answer. *Is this a spiritual Easter egg hunt?* I wondered. I'm sitting there asking my dad how he got from Point A to Point B, and he's telling me to go read the Bible. I could see that he wasn't going to say another word until I read Hebrews 11, so I hurried to my room to read it.

As you probably expected, I read through that passage like a wild man looking for the answer. As I did, the answer kept popping up over and over again.

It started with, "Now faith is the assurance of things hoped for, the conviction of things not seen. For by it the men of old gained approval" (vv. 1–2). Then it quickly went into calling each one out:

By faith we understand God spoke the world into existence . . .
(v. 3)

By faith Abel offered a better sacrifice . . . (v. 4)

By faith Enoch was taken up . . . (v. 5)

By faith Noah built an ark . . . (v. 7)

By faith Abraham obeyed . . . (v. 8)

By faith Sarah received the ability to conceive . . . (v. 11)

By faith Abraham offered up Isaac . . . (v. 17)

By faith Isaac blessed Jacob and Esau . . . (v. 20)

By faith Jacob blessed the sons of Joseph . . . (v. 21)

By faith Joseph mentioned the Exodus . . . (v. 22)

By faith Moses was hidden . . . (v. 23)

By faith Moses left Egypt . . . (v. 27)

By faith the Israelites passed through the Red Sea . . . (v. 29)

By faith the walls of Jericho fell down . . . (v. 30)

By faith Rahab did not perish, after she hid the spies . . . (v. 31)

Verse 32 starts with "And what more shall I say?" Then it goes on to name more people who did great things "by faith." People such as Gideon, Barak, Samson, Jephthah, David, Samuel. These people and more conquered kingdoms, obtained promises, shut the mouths of lions, and quenched the power of fire. In their weakness, they were made strong. In terrible battles, they became mighty men of war. They caused foreign armies to take flight. The list goes on and on. As verse 32 states, "And what more shall I say?" Nothing, really. Because that was enough. I now knew the answer to my dad's greatness. So I marched back into the living room to talk to him again. Sitting down, I said, "Dad, I know how you did it."

"How, son?" he asked.

"You did it by faith."

"Bingo, boy!" he exclaimed. "You got it." He then followed it up with his famous explanation of what faith is: "Faith is acting like it is so, even when it's not so, in order that it might be so, simply because God said so."

My teenage mind got stuck on that for a moment, though. That sounded good, but what did it mean, practically? So, I tried to figure it out myself. I asked him if it meant that I follow my heart. To which he was quick in his reply, "Son, I never said that. The heart is the most deceitful part of you and is desperately sick. Don't follow your heart. Instead, you live by faith in making your heart follow the truth. Once you learn to do that, you'll be just fine."

Living by faith means making your heart follow God's truth. When your desires, emotions, and responses to what life throws at you pull you one way, make sure you find out what God says about it and follow that. Walking by faith means giving up control over your choices. It means being obedient to what God has revealed to you. Yes, He has granted you free will. You get to make choices in life. But He also gets to decide when and to whom He unleashes His greatness.

Hot tip: God unleashes greatness on those who live by faith.

God is calling each of us to greatness in His kingdom. But we only get to experience it when we are willing to trust our very lives to the hands of our Father. We demonstrate this trust through actions of faith. We arrive at our promises by actions based on faith. Sure, we are saved for free, but spiritual maturity takes work. Salvation is a gift, but growth is a grind. You have to work at it. You have to obey what God tells you to do.

God has called you for greatness. He has a plan to unleash His greatness both in and through you. It's bigger than you because it's not just for you. That's important to realize. Because when I look at this culture today, it's one of the most narcissistic cultures ever. It's all about *me*. Every show, every podcast, every post is all about glorifying self. We chase greatness in this country for three people: me, myself, and I. But until you realize it's not all about you, God will allow you to stay settled in the sameness. He won't unleash you to go pursue all that is yours to have.

You need to understand that greatness doesn't mean storing up blessings for yourself. Greatness is all about increasing your influence and strength in such a way that you can become a greater blessing to others. God told Abraham He would make him a great nation first, then He said He'd make his name great. It wasn't the other way around. It was about the nation. It was about others. Abraham's name would become legendary, yes. But not until God's purpose of using him to bring blessing to others was carried out first.

But in our culture today, we've got it backwards. We want our name in lights first, before we'll agree to be the light of Christ to those who need it. We want our back scratched first, before we'll even scratch the surface in telling others what Jesus has come to do for them. We want our notoriety and crown on first, before we'll pay homage to the King who rules overall. But His kingdom doesn't work that way. That's the wrong direction. In fact, that sounds an awful lot like the direction of this world.

I was in chapel service a few years ago talking to the team, and I asked one of the players, "Who had your jersey number before you?" Then I asked if the name of that ex-Cowboy was still stitched across the back of the current player's uniform. He shook his head no.

"So," I continued, "will your name be stitched on the back of your Cowboys jersey when you move on or retire?" Of course his answer was no. I smiled, because I had made my point. See, far too frequently in our culture, we're chasing a greatness that is only good for a glimpse in time. We're working hard for a fame that is fleeting at best.

This reality hit me hard during one of the greatest challenges I have ever faced as a chaplain in the Cowboys organization. It came when one of the Cowboys players died the night before we flew to Cincinnati for an away game. Jerry Brown Jr. was killed in a car accident. On the morning of our departure, I was oblivious to the circumstances when I arrived at the airport.

I was walking up to the plane to get on with the players when I saw one of the coaches come off of the plane and indicate that he wanted to pull me aside. Because they had never pulled me aside in the five years I served as chaplain, I got nervous, thinking that maybe I was going to be the first NFL chaplain in league history to suddenly get cut. I instantly had a flashback to being cut when I was a player. That's how they do it. They just pull you aside and tell you to go home.

So as I stood there nervously waiting on the coach to say what he needed to say, he caught me by surprise, telling me that there had been a player death, then giving me the news about Jerry. Once he was done, he looked at me and made it clear that my play as the chaplain had been called: He wanted me to get on the plane and do something for the players.

I remember calling my dad really quick before getting on the plane. I wanted to ask him for advice. He told me to pray with them, console the guys, and be there for them, letting the Spirit move. I had planned on preaching on Ephesians 3 for the chapel service that night, but when I saw how many players showed up to chapel for the first time, the Spirit led me to change my message on a dime. It never fails. People show up to get answers when mortality kicks in because there's nowhere else to go for them. So I decided to preach on the Gospel instead. This was my opportunity to present the Gospel to the majority of the team. And, God be praised, a good number of the guys were saved that night.

It seemed to be going pretty smoothly that weekend, all things considered. But then it hit me. It was right when the game was about to start. We all stood on the sidelines for the national anthem and the announcements. Before it all started, the man on the loudspeaker acknowledged Jerry's death. He then said, "Let's give Jerry Brown Jr. a moment of silence." The whole stadium went quiet. For a moment. Then, we sang the anthem, the planes flew over, and they kicked the ball off. It all went by so fast.

When the pregame traditions concluded and the game was underway, I turned to the player next to me and said, "Is this what we're living for? Is this what you're playing for? You give the world years of your effort, skills, and talents, and all you get in return is a moment. Then, the game just continues." He just shook his head because in his heart, he understood.

But truth be told, that's all this world has to offer you. Hall of Famer or not, the most people are going to give you on this earth is a moment—if you even get that. Why? Because man can't offer anything else. We spend all this time chasing, grinding, working, struggling, and striving for worldly greatness and yet, when all is said and done, we get a moment of silence. That doesn't seem worth it to me. That's why living with an eternal perspective is so important. Because the greatness God has to offer you lasts a lot longer than a moment. God gives an eternity of blessings when you've reached your time to receive them. In addition to that, He gives you the opportunity to leave eternal impacts on other people's lives whom you influence for His good and His glory during your time on earth.

As we come to a close and reflect on Abraham's willingness to give up his comfortable life, his success, his notoriety, and go where God told him to go, I want to ask you to consider your own values. Are you living for a moment, by the world's standards? Are you living for what the culture will give you? Are you striving to be settled and comfortable only? Or are you living for true greatness? Are you willing to let go of all you know and pursue what God has for you?

I know you're probably chasing some stuff right now. I know you're pursuing your dreams. I know you have desires, ambitions, hopes, and goals for your life. And there's nothing wrong with that, unless it keeps you from allowing yourself to be unsettled when God calls your name. Unless it prevents you from letting God pull you, push you, and direct you to where you need to go. Only when you are willing to stop pushing back on God and truly allow faith to start pushing on you will you get the greatness He has in store for you. Only then will you see Him reach into His divine pocket and pull out the divine promise He's been wanting you to experience all along. Now . . . GO.

# CHAPTER 5

# DRESS

**It matters.** How you dress matters. You would never think of wearing a wool suit to the beach or a pair of shorts to go ice skating. If you are getting married, you don't get dressed like you are going to the gym. If you are graduating from college and getting an award, you are not going to dress like you are going to the movies. What you wear reflects where you are headed. It can also reflect who you are.

A football team's uniform identifies the players as belonging to that team. A doctor's white coat signifies his or her role. Every Tuesday at the church where my Dad pastors and I have the honor of working as well, the men wear button-up shirts and a tie. It's "meeting day," and the tradition of wearing a tie for meetings has stayed strong all these years (despite many attempts to loosen it)!

What we wear matters. It says something. It means something. It makes a statement. Similarly, what you wear in the spiritual realm matters too. If it didn't, then Paul would not have told us how to get dressed for battle (see Ephesians 6:10–20).

Likewise, if you want to get what God is giving you, you have to be dressed in connection with how great that purpose, promise, and destiny truly is.

The Bible says a lot about what we wear. One verse in particular may be so familiar to you that the meaning behind it could have gotten lost. I know that happens to me when I read over something I've read before. I end up skimming it while missing out on the meat of it. But not too long ago when I was reading Genesis 3, the chapter this verse is in, I stopped as I read it. A light bulb went off. I couldn't get beyond this one verse, verse 21, because it captivated me.

This passage gave me pause because it stood out to me as never before. I had to sit with it a minute as I did my devotions because so much spoke to me from this one short verse. It says, "The LORD God made garments of skin for Adam and his wife, and clothed them."

Now, you may be thinking, *Why would this verse give me pause? Why would this verse stand out in a chapter full of intrigue and drama? Why 21, Jonathan?* The reason is simple. As I read over this statement in Scripture, I started to wonder why God felt the need to re-clothe someone who was already dressed. Ever thought about that?

Adam and Eve were already dressed. We saw that in verse 7 earlier in the chapter. They had gotten creative once they realized they were naked and sewn some fig leaves together. So why would God clothe someone who was already clothed?

As I thought about it some more, I realized that God didn't clothe them because they were naked. He gave them new clothes to put on because He didn't like how they were dressed. He didn't care for what they had on. There was something insufficient about what the two of them had sewn together and gotten into that just didn't sit right with God.

If you think about it like this, you can see God coming through the Garden like a stylist. He's walking through in the cool of the day as

He normally did. Then He sees Adam and Eve who are now, in their minds, dressed to the nines. They've gone and covered themselves with the best of the plant leaves around them. Now, God must have been unsatisfied with what He saw because he did a double take. God saw what they were wearing and shook His head.

If you use your imagination just a bit, you might even see it play out. God comes walking along. He spots the two of them dressed in fig leaves and so He says, "What y'all got on?"

They might look up at Him at that point, wondering what's wrong with how they are dressed. Maybe they become self-conscious and try to pat it down a bit where the leaves are sticking out or didn't get stitched just right. But God doesn't care about anything being patted down. He's not interested in their stitching skills. He's disappointed in the whole outfit. So, He continues His one-way conversation with the two of them,

"Where do you think you're going in that?"

You've probably heard this said to you at some point yourself. Could have been by your parents. Might have been your spouse. A friend or sibling, even. Or maybe you've said it to your kids. You know exactly what the question means. It can be translated easily into the statement

"You aren't going anywhere in that."

Maybe God wanted them to contemplate the insufficiency of their wardrobe before He gave them new threads. Maybe you can imagine Him adding the line, "What you have on does not match where you are headed." Then He proceeded to give them a change of clothes.

It's just one verse but it gives us a life principle that, if we apply it, can change the whole outcome of our story. God needed to change Adam and Eve's clothes because they were not wearing the true covering they needed in order to go where God was taking them. They were wearing something, sure. But they weren't wearing something that was conducive to the environment to which they were headed.

There are many Christians today who are claiming Christianity as their own yet wearing the wrong clothes. They are claiming to be followers of Christ but are improperly dressed. They claim kingdom allegiance, but *how* they are dressed wouldn't even get them in the King's front door. All the while they wonder why God isn't taking them where He wants them to go. They are upset and disappointed that they have not yet gotten all that God has in store for them to have.

But God is simply telling us all through this one short but powerful verse that the reason you haven't gotten what He has for you yet is because *how* you are dressed determines *how far* you go. It determines whether or not you get in to where you are trying to go. You must be dressed for the occasion or venue.

Yes, you're wearing something, but it's not the something He has for you to put on.

Please understand that God cares about what you are wearing. All through the Bible He addresses what a person wears. If you go through Matthew 22 and read the parable of the wedding feast, you'll see that in it Jesus returns for His second coming. He comes back to wed His bride, the church. His Father, the King, invites some guests to the wedding reception. But one of the people invited shows up in the wrong clothes. He's improperly dressed. Now, this man isn't pulled to the side and politely told to go borrow a jacket or that there is an extra one for him in the cloak room he can grab. That might be how you or I would handle the situation. However, Jesus handles it His own way because He's Jesus. He tells the story like this:

"Friend, how did you come in here without wedding clothes?" And the man was speechless. Then the king said to the servants, "Bind him hand and foot, and throw him into the outer darkness; in that place there will be weeping and gnashing of teeth." For many are called, but few are chosen.

vv. 12–14

You can picture the King at the entrance, standing there with his hands on his hips. He's shaking his head. It's possible he could get the whole question out in one breath: How on earth do you think you're getting in dressed like that?

Or, it could be simply a gesture to his clothes and another shaking of His head. The King doesn't have time for a lot of words because the line to get in is so long already. So He turns the man away. There's no cloakroom hand-me-down for this man. Instead, he is thrown into the outer darkness. And not just any outer darkness. This is the place where weeping and gnashing of teeth is going on. Why was he tossed there? Because he did not dress for the occasion.

The King banished him there because somehow the man thought it would be okay to come to the wedding feast without the right outfit on. His choice just wasn't going to cut it. The King had a dress code, and if someone decided not to go by the dress code, they were shown the door.

The King had every right to do that because it was His wedding feast. He was footing the bill, running the show, and making the rules. Just as God had every right to re-clothe Adam and Eve in the garden.

These verses remind me of a time when my wife and I were going on a date early on in our marriage. Now, keep in mind, she married an athlete. What that means is when it comes to dressing, I just want to be comfortable. Just give me some basketball shorts and a T-shirt. I can dress that up with a nice pair of Jordans. That's all I need to make it pop. I'm not into all of the extras. I can easily walk out of the house dressed in athletic clothes and call it a date night. No problem at all.

You can probably see where this is going. It was about time for us to get ready for our date when Kanika turned to me and said, "Time to get dressed."

I said, "How much time we got?"

She said, "About forty minutes."

I shot back, "Call me when we're down to ten minutes because that's all the time I need." I was thinking that was more than enough time to put on a clean pair of basketball shorts and pick out a new T-shirt.

Kanika stopped in her tracks. She gave me a lingering look. Then said, "Jonathan, can you please come in here? We should go ahead and get dressed so we're not late."

I shrugged it off and said okay. After I went in and got dressed in my shorts and shirt, I came out to find her combing her hair. Kanika took one look at me and stopped combing altogether. She just stopped and looked. Now, my wife has two facial expressions she can give you. She'll either smile at you with the top row of teeth showing, or she will smile and show both rows of teeth. I quickly learned in our relationship that the smile with two sets of teeth isn't actually a smile. It's more like a look of concern. You might be able to guess which smile I got when she said, "Oh, is that what you're wearing?"

I was like, "Yes, this is what I am wearing. It's what I have on. Is that a leading question?"

Kanika didn't even bother to answer. Instead she just walked into the closet, moved me to the side, picked out a button-up shirt, got some nice jeans, and grabbed some dress shoes. She laid them all out and said, "Can you please put this on?"

I said, "Okay," but then asked, "Why do I have to change my clothes?"

To which she replied, "Because what you are wearing is not conducive to where we are going." Then she threw her head back and walked out to finish getting ready. I just stood there having had it handed to me good. She was right. Kanika was right. And I needed to get in alignment with the program at hand.

I want to ask you the same question as we spend time together in this book. Is what you are wearing conducive to where you are going? Does what you have on align with where your story is headed? There are too many believers dressed like heathens today. And God takes one look at them and says, "You look good to you, and you even look good to other people, but I'm showing you both sets of teeth right now because you don't look good to Me. You're not dressed for where your story is headed."

## Dress for Success

It's amazing to me that Adam and Eve went into their worldly environment to find their covering. It never dawned on them to go to the God whom they offended to make sure they were properly covered. They chose to chase after the world in covering themselves instead of going to the God who made the world. But Adam and Eve's story isn't much different from many of our own. There are many Christians chasing after what the environment has to offer so they can look good to themselves and to those around them, all the while kicking God to the curb.

Adam and Eve were satisfied with the fig leaves they had found. They thought they had turned their issue into a non-issue all by themselves. They figured out how to outwardly present a covering. They thought that it would be enough if they showed the right face. They covered their shame. But God wasn't impressed with their sewing skills, and neither is He impressed with ours.

It's sad to say this but it's true—we've become professionals in this culture of showing the right face. We've become professionals in this culture at knowing how to dress for "likes" and for more people to follow us. We want to be liked. We want to hear the compliments. We want everybody to see our pictures and what we have on. "Look at me," we say through our selfies, all the while trying to downplay our posts by captioning, "I woke up like this." Yeah right! You know you spent an hour on that photo and smoothed it, edited it, filtered it. But, right. You think we really believe you woke up like that? We're not buying that, and neither is God.

We've become professionals at wearing costumes that impress the world, all the while ignoring the fact that God is not fooled or impressed. He's showing us both sets of His teeth.

In fact, because of the culture we live in, many people have figured out how to dress nicely from a dirty closet. What's more, we seem to think that simply because people are liking our pictures, or people are applauding us, or people are saying, "Oh, you look nice!" that we're doing it well. We're hearing things like "Good job." Good career. Good house. Good car. Good hair. Good hat. Good clothes. And because we're hearing these things day in and day out, we are starting to believe them. We are starting to believe, as a culture, that just showing up at church is enough, as long as we can use a social media "check-in" to prove we were there. We are starting to believe, as a culture, that just attending small groups or special events is enough, as long as we can post a group pic and tag our location. When it comes to being a Christian, we are slowly going down the rabbit hole of finding our value in looking the part rather than actually being the part. We are starting to believe, as a culture, that the applause of humanity equals the applause of God.

But I am here to remind you about something critical right now: The two are not synonymous.

Yet it's hard to remember this truth in the culture we live in. That our true allegiance needs to be to God instead of humanity is not reinforced on the daily. If I could be straight up with you, there are men I know who show up to church dressed to the nines ready to serve in ministry who simultaneously do not love their wives. Rest assured, they'll be at church on time. They'll button up their shirts just right. They'll say their long-drawn-out super-churchy prayers, join the leadership team, and even become deacons. They'll do all of these things and everyone around them will think they're doing great spiritually. But if you were to sit down and talk with them, as I have, you'd know it's just a cover. It's an attempt to edit their spiritual rags by selecting a designer Christian filter. They have everyone thinking one thing, but God is thinking another. God is coming into their garden in the cool of the day asking, "What on earth do you have on?"

As I reflected on this verse that held me in its grips during my devotional time, I started to look at the closet of my own heart. I started to ask myself the questions I was asking about Adam and Eve. I started to examine whether I was living a filtered Christian life, or a real one. Was I chasing what the world had to offer or was I chasing after the One who made the world?

It gave me pause to wonder. Do I check on my likes more than I check on my wife? Do I spend so much time trying to raise my status in the world that my status is dropping with my kids? Do I work to get people to follow me more than I do to get them to follow Christ?

Even now, as I'm thinking about the fig leaves I may have sewn together, I'm starting to wonder what in the world I have on. How did I ever come to believe that the world's clothes would get me into kingdom locations?

What about you? Are you climbing the ladder of success only to get to the top and realize that the whole time it's been leaning against the wrong wall? How many of us will be successful and unsuccessful all at the same time, sewing together a life that looks good to one another, but not to God? Adam and Eve looked good to one another; they had no complaints with the garments they had sewn together. Meanwhile, God was on His way with a whole new outfit to let them know that what worked for them would not work for Him. They met each other's expectations while sorely missing His.

I have to give it to them, though: Adam and Eve tried hard; I have no doubt. They carefully chose what to wear. The Bible specifically tells us it was fig leaves.

Fig leaves are large leaves. If you ever want to get some shade from the sun, sit under a fig tree. Fig leaves are also strong. They aren't easily torn. In fact, shoppers in marketplaces in the Middle East in the past had their purchases wrapped up in a fig leaf to carry them home. People would carry their fruits or spices or nuts in fig leaves because these leaves are large and strong. They would even wrap gifts in fig leaves and tie them up with a bow. Fig leaves look that good. Adam and Eve didn't just pull any old leaves off of a tree

Are you climbing the ladder of success only to get to the top and realize that the whole time it's been leaning against the wrong wall? How many of us will be successful and unsuccessful all at the same time, sewing together a life that looks good to one another, but not to God?

and start sewing. Rather, they chose what was large, valuable, and strong. And don't we do the same?

We show everyone our house, if it's large. We show everyone our car, if it's valuable. We show everyone pictures of us working out, if we're strong. We give impressions of what we know (or think) will impress. Why? Because it makes us feel better about ourselves, like Adam and Eve felt better about themselves all dressed up in their fig leaves.

Never mind that our large house has never become a home. Never mind that we're struggling to pay the note on this way-too-expensive car. Never mind that we are neglecting our spiritual exercises so that we can increase our muscle mass. Never mind that our fig leaves have become a personal obsession for our ego so that we can cover our shame and inadequacies with pride. Never mind all of that. Because when the world is liking and applauding, God's approval of how we're dressed doesn't mean much anymore.

But then we complain that we can't seem to get all that God has in store for us. To which He replies, "I can't give it to you. I don't like what you have on."

The solution is to go to the God who knows how to cover us with what we should be wearing. Because when the waters of life get rough and the boat gets shaky, fig leaves aren't going to be enough. We see this in Genesis 3 because even though Adam and Eve had taken the time to cover themselves up, they still hid from God when He came looking for them. They were covered, but deep down they still felt naked. They were clothed, but they still felt shame. They were dressed, but they still felt discouraged, depressed, and on their own.

That being so, we might wonder why they tried to cover themselves at all. Probably the same reason we do. We seek to cover up that which can only be covered through obedience to God. Because when Adam and Eve were obedient, they were naked but unashamed. They felt the covering of obedience. When they were disobedient, they clothed themselves but were still ashamed. They recognized just how naked they really were.

There is a covering of protection that is simply tied to faith in Christ and allegiance to His overarching rule in your life. It's embedded into obedience. Faith in Christ saves you, but once you add disobedience to the equation of your relationship with God, you get that naked feeling again. Once you see your wrongful actions boomerang right back to slap you in the face, you feel naked and vulnerable. You may be rich through illegitimate gain in your finances, but you're sweating the whole time. You may be sleeping around to get pleasure, but it's not pleasurable having to wait on the results to find out if something got passed around. You may be enjoying what the world has to offer, but you're simultaneously running from what God wants to give. When Adam and Eve went away from the Father to do things their own way, they paid the price—in more ways than one.

My seven-year-old son, Kamden, is my mini-me. When he was a toddler, I was holding him as we walked out of a restaurant one day and a lady said to me, "Don't divorce your wife, because you'll definitely have to pay child support for that one! He looks just like you!" He inherited a lot of my traits, but he has a much stronger will than I ever had. Strong enough to motivate him to start walking at eight months old. Plus, he's got energy enough for a few kids, and he likes to do things his way. If you follow me or my wife on social media, he's the one you see swinging from the chandeliers or climbing a tree, hence the reason we nicknamed him "Spider-Kam." Because of his constant quest for adventure mixed with a lack of fear, we had to put a baby gate up on the stairs much earlier for him than with our other kids.

But eventually it came time for the baby gate to come down and for Kamden to learn how to walk down the stairs. In an effort to teach him, I grabbed hold of his hand. He was still under two so he couldn't get down the stairs on his own. But he didn't care. As we descended together one step at a time, he continuously attempted to yank his hand free of my grip. All the while I kept saying, "Kamden, Kamden—you can't go down these stairs by yourself."

Kamden wasn't listening to me. He just kept on yanking his hand to break free. He wanted to go down the stairs on his own. Eventually we made it near the bottom of the stairs. We had one step left and I decided this was my opportunity to teach Kamden a lesson that would help him in the long run. He had been trying to break free of my hand the whole way down, but it would have been dangerous for me to let go early on. Yet with one step left, I knew I could release him. So I did. Kamden's face lit up, just before he tumbled down that one final stair. He ended up on his butt all because he insisted on going at it alone, his own way.

Sometimes God will let us do that too. We try our own way. We choose our own way. We want our own way. So He lets us learn the hard way. He lets go of our hand, and we fall flat on our butts too. Yes, we have free will. God can't make us believe His way is better. He will let us have our way so that we will learn not to yank away from Him and His will.

As Kamden sat at the bottom of the stairs, now crying, he knew full well whose hand he should have held on to. I'm certain that he knew because every time after that, when it came time for him to go down the stairs, he reached out his hand to grab mine. He came straight to me if he wanted to go down. And it's the same way with us. We find ourselves vulnerable because we've yanked ourselves away from God's path. Or we've sought to cover up our shame with the world's values. But if we just turn around, we'll see His hand still there. We'll see our Daddy right there waiting to pick us back up, dust us off, and get us clothed in what He knows to be best.

Let me explain something really quick. If someone tells you life is purposeless, you have to assume that purpose exists. You can't have purposelessness without first having purpose. There is no meaning in the term if you and I weren't created for purpose first. Or, as another example, if you are put in a dark world without eyes to see, the darkness would have no meaning to you. The only reason darkness signifies is because you were made for the light. Adam and Eve recognized they had been created for righteousness precisely because of their sin. They realized their shame because of the shamelessness they had once known. They knew they had to be covered in order to feel secure and protected because they had felt secure and protected by God himself.

The problem with Adam and Eve wasn't that they didn't know about sin or what they had done wrong. The problem was that they ran to the world to fix it. They ran to their environment for righteousness. They tried to cover themselves with that which was never designed to cover them.

We do the same. We present a great face to try to make others believe we're righteous and clean. We filter our words as much as we filter our photos to make sure we sound on point. We'll even defend ourselves when we're wrong because deep down inside we know we have been created to do right, and we want to believe we are doing it. We've been created for righteousness. We've been created for purpose. We've been created to make a difference for good in this land.

But going to the world for righteousness is no different than going to water to dry off. Both your direction and your action have just contradicted what you were put here for. Regardless, we still wind up chasing the world because the world is what we can see. We like the world. We want the world. We smile for the camera while wearing the world. All the while God is showing us both sets of teeth and wondering *how* in the world we can wear the world and simultaneously expect a destiny from the kingdom. God is walking through our gardens seeing what we are wearing and saying to himself, *How?*

What made God's garments acceptable while Adam and Eve's were not is obvious, but I want to draw our attention to it before we close this chapter. In Genesis 2:17 God told Adam and Eve that the day they ate the fruit from the forbidden tree, they would surely die. But they didn't surely die right then. Adam went on to live over 900 years. But eventually he did die because of sin. The body is contaminated, so the body has to be put to death. Yet the reason he didn't die right then in the garden was because of a promise from God. The Lord God made garments of skin and clothed them.

In the garden was the first sacrifice. God didn't get those skins from a skin tree. God performed a sacrifice in the garden. He took the skins off of the animal, or perhaps even animals, and placed the skins on Adam and Eve. They were to serve as a constant reminder that the only reason they were still alive was because the innocent lamb died in their place.

Likewise, we are covered because of the shed blood of Jesus Christ, and our clothing should reflect that reality. That is, our lifestyle should reflect the sacrifice that was made on our behalf. The only reason you and I are here today is because we are a living testimony of the innocent Lamb who was slain. So when you or I take off His skins and put on our own threads instead, it's an insult to the One who gave His all so that we could legitimately be dressed to impress for the occasion of our kingdom destiny.

Our lifestyle should reflect the sacrifice that was made on our behalf. The only reason you and I are here today is because we are a living testimony of the innocent Lamb who was slain. So when you or I take off His skins and put on our own threads instead, it's an insult to the One who gave His all so that we could legitimately be dressed to impress for the occasion of our kingdom destiny.

As I look at the testimony of the generations who have come before me and as I consider the truth of how Christ's sacrifice covers me, I know the only way I can move forward and go to the place God is calling me to go has to do with how I choose to dress. It has to do with whether or not what I wear is what He wants me to wear. Isaiah 61:10 explains it this way: "I will rejoice greatly in the Lord, my soul will exult in my God; for He has clothed me with garments of salvation, He has wrapped me with a robe of righteousness, as a bridegroom decks himself with a garland, and as a bride adorns herself with her jewels."

*Your Time Is Now* to go with God to the place of your calling, purpose, and destiny.

But He will only take you when you are ready to fully understand what you are to wear in order to get there. You are to wear an abiding surrender to His Son Jesus Christ. He is the One who clothes you as you are to be clothed in order to get all God has given you. Jesus is the One. Through His sacrifice, He has shown each of us how we are to . . . *DRESS.*

# CHAPTER 6

# CONFIDENCE

**What do you think of when you hear the word *confidence*?** Do you think of someone who has it all together? Do you think of Tom Brady with two minutes left, down by a few points, in the Super Bowl? Do you think of the images of perfect-looking people you scroll past on social media? Confidence means a lot of different things to different people. But oftentimes, if you were to peel back the veneer of what our world defines as *confidence*, you'll find it's just a mask. It's just an image to hide an insecurity. Or it's just a motivation and drive to avoid failure. Having known celebrities and elite athletes personally, I can tell you this firsthand.

Confidence often camouflages uncertainty.

But when it comes to confidence in Scripture, we're talking a whole other ball game. Why? Because confidence rests on who you are putting that confidence in. If it's in yourself, you're going to find out at one time or another, you aren't all that you might have thought you were. You're going to let yourself down. We all do. We're human.

Or, if you put confidence in another person you've placed on a pedestal, watch out. Pedestals crash and crumble. They aren't as sturdy as you might think. Even if you put your confidence in a tradition or belief system, you will soon learn that these have holes when not rooted and founded on the entirety of God's written Word—and most are not.

Only when you put your confidence in God have you chosen that which will stand up to the challenge. The Bible reminds us of this time and again:

> For the LORD will be your confidence and will keep your foot from being caught.
>
> Proverbs 3:26

> Therefore let us draw near with confidence to the throne of grace, so that we may receive mercy and find grace to help in time of need.
>
> Hebrews 4:16

> So that we confidently say, "THE LORD IS MY HELPER, I WILL NOT BE AFRAID. WHAT WILL MAN DO TO ME?"
>
> Hebrews 13:6

> This is the confidence which we have before Him, that, if we ask anything according to His will, He hears us.
>
> 1 John 5:14

Another way to define the word *confidence*, biblically, is assurance. I like to say it's when "you know that you know that you know." You can count on whatever it is you are assured of or about. Hebrews 11:1 puts it like this: "Now faith is the assurance of things hoped for, the conviction of things not seen." Confidence and assurance can be summarized as a conviction that what you believe to be true *is* true—or the person you believe to be solid *is* solid. Your level of confidence always affects your actions.

You have probably heard it said about an athlete or a team that seems to lack confidence that they "choke" at the end of a game. This lack of confidence in themselves and in each other shows up in what they do and how they play. They may stand as though they are confident. They could even look like they are confident. But most of the time that is just to try to convince themselves of a confidence they don't truly own.

True confidence doesn't need to be displayed. It requires no bravado. It just shows up in the consistent ability of the one who has to do the right thing, make the play, secure the deal, ride out the storm, or maneuver through life's difficulties and challenges. True confidence is knowing that the one in whom confidence is placed—be it yourself or another—will hold up to the expectations at hand.

With that in mind, we will see that in the next Scripture we are going to examine, Paul is essentially giving us the secret to what we all seek. He tells us how to get all that God has given to each of us. And you'll see it's not rocket science. In fact, I imagine that most of you reading this book have the verse memorized. It might be a saying embedded in your soul. But just because you know something doesn't mean you truly *know* it, so we're going to dig deeper right now. Paul writes in Philippians 1:6,

> For I am confident of this very thing, that He who began a good work in you will perfect it until the day of Christ Jesus.

He wants us to know that God *will* perfect what He started in everyone who trusts Him.

Now, Paul starts out his statement by talking about this thing called confidence, which we addressed earlier. The reason he starts out with confidence is so that we are reminded that his confidence is not rooted in himself. His confidence is connected to that in which he has placed it. The object of Paul's confidence is "He." It's not "me," himself. It's not Paul. Paul knows that the He who began the good work is his Savior. He also knows that his Savior is worthy of his confidence.

A lot of times our expectations are not met or we get thrown off track in life because our confidence is misplaced in something other than God. Sometimes our confidence is in things that cannot be held responsible for the valuable beliefs we're giving to the object of our confidence. It might be that we misplace our confidence in people. Other times we misplace confidence in things and places. I know we often misplace it in ourselves and our own ability to overcome the circumstances we are going through or to achieve what we want. Yet when it comes to placing our confidence in something from a spiritual perspective, anything other than God is a false god. It's not going to come through for you. And if that false god is you, *you're* not going to come through for you. Not in the spiritual realm.

Sure, you may be great at lifting weights or strategizing the growth of your business. You might know how to be an awesome parent or community leader. But when it comes to going after all that God has in store for you, that's a spiritual thing. Putting all your eggs in any basket other than God himself will do only one thing for you: teach you not to do that again. Because when it fails, you'll realize that in the spiritual life, it is only God who deserves—and has earned—your confidence.

Paul has confidence in an appropriate Object worthy of the assurance he has in it. One of the biggest reasons people waste so much time living outside of God's plan for their lives is because they are placing their confidence in the wrong thing. They are placing

Putting all your eggs in any basket other than God himself will do only one thing for you: teach you not to do that again. Because when it fails, you'll realize that in the spiritual life, it is only God who deserves—and has earned—your confidence.

it in their career, their family members, relationships, money, or even their own abilities. And while we naturally have a tendency to place confidence in other people, our plans, and our own abilities for navigating the daily grind, that is not what gets us to the goal spiritually. Too many people are confused about this.

By the end of this book, you're probably going to think I only have one kid—Kamden. But I actually have five. The reason you'll probably think I only have one kid is because Kamden—you know, Spider-Kam—usually gives me all of my illustrations. He's enough for any Bible teacher to fill a book with examples! Case in point, one day after plopping down on my big, comfy couch ready to watch some college football, I decided to give Kamden my phone. My battery was almost out. I was feeling lazy. So I gave my son the phone and said, "Kamden, I need you to put my phone on my bedside table and plug it in for me. I know you know how to do it because you're five now. So go and take this phone and plug it in for me because it's running out of juice."

It seemed as though he understood my instructions by the expression registered on his face—he had a twinkle in his eye as he stared at me without blinking. He nodded. He was totally focused. So I handed my phone to him with confidence. He ran off with my phone with a bit of pride in his step and that's the last I saw of Kamden for a while. A little bit later, I went looking for my phone and discovered that it wasn't on my bedside table where I expected it to be. Puzzled, I went searching for Kamden. When I found him playing in the playroom with his younger sister without a care in the world, I said, "Kamden, where is my phone?"

Kamden replied, "I don't know."

To which I responded as any rational parent would, "What do you mean you don't know? I just told you fifteen minutes ago to put my phone on my bedside table and plug it in. So where is my phone? It's not there."

Kamden started to stammer a bit, taken aback by the urgency of my question, "I-I-I don't know, Daddy. I forgot."

"You forgot?" I asked. "It was fifteen minutes ago. Son, I told you to put my phone on my bedside table. What do you mean, you 'forgot'?"

You can see where this is going. Nowhere. So as I was talking to Kamden, my wife started talking to me. She's giving me "the look" too. Kanika said, "Jonathan, you do realize you're talking to a five-year-old?"

"Yes, I know that. That's my son," I shot back.

She just continued, still with the look: "You do realize that he's not the problem?"

I shook my head, confused. So she went on, "You gave something valuable to someone who is irresponsible and now you're mad at the one you gave it to when you never should have given it to him to begin with. He's five years old. He's not the problem."

I'll admit, I got a little hot inside as Kanika was pointing this out to me, but there was nothing I could say, because I knew deep down she was right. Why in the world would I give something valuable to someone irresponsible and then get mad when irresponsibility inevitably shows up. My confidence was misplaced and so was my frustration.

With this humbling realization I began the search for my phone. Alone. Because I was the one who misplaced my confidence and therefore misplaced my phone. Spider-Kam lost it, but it was up to me to find it. So let the frustrating and daunting search begin. 😊😊

A lot of times, though, that's just what we all do. We give the value of our confidence, the value of our faith, or the value of our trust to things and people who should not be held responsible for it. We give it to those who are unable to take us where God wants us to be. Then we get mad when they disappoint us. We get mad when things don't work out, or when people aren't doing what we wanted them to do. But we're getting mad for all the wrong reasons and at all the wrong people, because when things aren't operating the way they're supposed to be operating, it's often due to the fact that we misplaced our hope in that which didn't deserve it.

Paul tells us in Hebrews 12 that he is confident because of God. Paul is confident in He, not me. Paul is confident in Him, not them. Paul is confident in our Savior, not in any person, place, thing, or thought. Paul knows that the One who started the good work taking place in his life will finish it. The One who began the journey of our soul will complete it. The One who initiated the spiritual growth will ensure it comes to its full fruition. Paul knows this because he knows the One he's talking about. He knows Him like the author of Hebrews 12:2 knows Him when he writes,

> Fixing our eyes on Jesus, the author and perfecter of faith, who for the joy set before Him endured the cross, despising the shame, and has sat down at the right hand of the throne of God.

We are to fix our eyes on Jesus because He is the author and perfecter of our faith. We can be confident He will do what He says He will do because we know that Jesus perfects what He starts. That's why Paul could so assuredly write Romans 8:28–29 as wisdom for us to live by, because he knew that Jesus was involved. And when Jesus is in the picture, that changes everything. Paul confidently penned,

> And we know that God causes all things to work together for good to those who love God, to those who are called according to His

purpose. For those whom He foreknew, He also predestined to become conformed to the image of His Son, so that He would be the firstborn among many brethren.

Those He predestined, He already called. Those He called, He already justified. Those He justified, He glorified. That's why we can say, as Paul writes in verse 31, that if and when God is for us, who in the world can be against us? If God is for you, who can be against you? Some may rise up to appear like they are against you, but the point is, who of any credibility, skill, or real damaging ability can be against you? No one. Nothing. If God is for you, you don't need to be tripping over the situation that you are going through. If God is for you, you don't need to be anxious about the life challenge you are facing. If God is for you, you don't need to worry about the circumstances and trials that test you. Because if you have faith in Jesus as your "finisher," you can let go of any fears of your future.

When I want to watch football during the off-season, I always turn to NFL Network—specifically NFL Replay. NFL Replay is a good way to experience football year-round. The difference with viewing these games is that I already know the outcomes of the games at kickoff. I already know who is going to win and who is going to lose because it was already determined during the regular season. Therefore, I'm able to view the games with a whole different level of confidence.

That's why if there is an interception, I don't end up fussing. If there's a fumble, I'm not getting worried. If someone on the team I'm cheering for misses a tackle, I'm not sulking. While those are bad things to happen during a game, if I already know the score and I already know my team wins, then why would I get caught up in the problems along the way? I can watch the victories with confidence because I already know how it finishes.

When Paul tells us that he is confident that He who began a good work in you will complete it, he is reminding us that we already know how this thing called life winds up. For those who trust in Christ and live by His plans, it finishes well. That's why Jesus could say with ease, "These things I have spoken to you, so that in Me you may have peace. In the world you have tribulation, but take courage; I have overcome the world" (John 16:33).

In today's translation, "Chill. Settle down. I got this."

Even through the fumbles, interceptions, or missed tackles in the game of your life, you can rest because you already know who the Overcomer truly is. What's more, you know that He is in you (Colossians 1:27).

You remember my boy Joshua, right? We started this book by looking at him. One part of his life that stands out to me most is when God told him, "Every place on which the sole of your foot treads, I have given it to you" (Joshua 1:3). Everywhere Joshua went, he was already assured of the victory. Everywhere Joshua walked, it was his to have. He had already been blessed. He had already gotten the victory. He had already been told how his game would wind up. Why wouldn't he walk with confidence then? Why wouldn't he be willing to go with whatever route God called, no matter how weird it might have sounded? Joshua knew the outcome, so he went out and got all that God had planned for him.

People often say to me, as a chaplain and pastor, "Jonathan, you don't know what I'm going through, though. You don't understand what I'm dealing with. You don't get how hard this is." Now first off, I have been through some trying times in my life, so try me, because I probably do understand. But secondly, even if I don't personally understand how hard it is or how difficult the challenges are that you may face, I am confident that He who brought you to this place will take you through it. He who put you in the position you are in will be faithful to perfect you in it. He who began the good work in you will not just leave you hanging out there on your own. I know this because I am confident we are dealing with a Finisher. Not only that, but we are dealing with a Finisher who is faithful.

## The Good News of the Good Work

So what is the good work Paul writes about being so confident in? What is it that God wants to bring about in you? The good work is the Good News. It's the Gospel of Jesus Christ. God sent His own Son to first live a perfect life, then die on the cross and resurrect three days later. He did this for me and you. This is the good work He's working out through you. Now, if you're saved, you might be scratching your head and wondering what this means. It means the good works you will do are not reliant on you. Jesus will bring them about when you have placed your hope and your faith in Him. It takes the pressure off of you.

In Exodus 20, God gave the Israelites the Ten Commandments. These commandments outlined what every sinner needed to do in order to be in a right relationship with God. But you know as well as I do that no one can obey those laws perfectly, just as no one can obey the more than 600 statutes and ordinances that were later tacked on to them. It was evident to God that humanity couldn't keep up with His perfect standard. So He sent the One who could. He sent His Son, Jesus Christ, to live out the perfect standard of God's law. That's why Jesus tells us in Matthew 5:17, "Do not think that I came to abolish the Law or the Prophets; I did not come to abolish but to fulfill."

You'll find as you read the Gospels that Jesus came to fulfill the law so that God's standard could be satisfied. As 2 Corinthians 5:21

says, "He made Him who knew no sin to be sin on our behalf, so that we might become the righteousness of God in Him." Not only did Jesus live perfectly, but He also died perfectly so that He could rise perfectly from the grave. That is a receipt to let you and me know that the price has been paid in full. As a result, we get to experience His perfection in this life. We don't get the death that we deserve because He took that death in our place. His good work sets the marker for all of our good works to come.

When Paul writes that he is confident that Christ, who began the greatest of good works in you, will carry it through to completion, he is reminding you of just how far you have already come. You can be confident because the greatest work of all time is just the starting gun. When you know that God looks at you and sees His Son residing in you and the work He has already done for you, you are assured of His love and His ability to do even more through you on this earth. If He's already done so much, there are no limits to what God wants to do both in and through you for His kingdom and His glory.

Jesus has freely given you salvation, just for believing. But while salvation is free, sanctification is not. Yes, God wants you to be saved, but He also wants you to be sanctified. *Sanctification* is just a seminary-style word that means spiritual growth. Don't trip on it. God has given you perfection through Jesus Christ, but God is still in the process of perfecting you to be like Jesus Christ on earth (1 Corinthians 11:1). To receive Christ's eternal perfection through trusting in Him by faith alone is called justification. Justification is a law court term. It means a verdict has been rendered on your behalf. It refers to the Judge looking at you and declaring that you are justified, not guilty, free to go. But what you need to understand is that justification is a gift, while sanctification is a grind. Justification means you are sinless in the eyes of God, but sanctification means that you progressively sin *less* because of the work of God in your life.

Justification might be compared to being drafted to a team. Sanctification determines how much playing time you get on the team that drafts you. And your playing time is determined by how much work you put in—your effort. It involves your execution. See, most people want the gift. They want the contract. But they're not interested in the grind. God says that He justifies us for free, but sanctification requires our cooperation and participation. It requires leveling up. But while it requires our action, God assures us that if we do it according to His will and His ways, He will see us through. He is faithful to work out the perfection that was already worked in when we accepted Christ.

Paul reminds us in this passage that even though you and I can't lose our salvation, it's important for us to focus on matching our lifestyle to our salvation. We do this with thoughts, decisions, words, desires, and ambitions aligned with Christ.

Yet keep in mind that because we are sinners with selfish ways, often what sharpens our spiritual skills and matures our muscles comes through difficulties and trials. God "perfects" us through the hardships of life.

Now, I have an idea what you might be wondering, because it wouldn't be the first time I've gotten this response when I share these truths. You might be thinking, *But Jonathan, how long is this gonna take?*

My answer is the same as Paul's. It's going to take "until the day of Christ Jesus." And no one knows how long that will be until that day comes. It's an indefinite day. That's why we should never quit. None of us will ever arrive in this life. One trophy isn't enough. One crown isn't enough. One victory isn't enough. One great play isn't enough. This entire life is about the process of God taking you through things in order to perfect you for His glory.

That's why Philippians 2:12 says that each of us is to work out our own salvation in fear and trembling. It doesn't say to work *for* our salvation, but to work it *out*. You've been given salvation through the sacrifice of Christ. But it's your role now to work out what God has already worked in. You work in concert with Him to attain the perfection Jesus has placed within.

I can assume that since you picked up this book, you're probably going through some stuff. You're facing some challenges. You've hit some brick walls. You want to know how to break through and reach that place of end-zone dances and celebrations. I understand that. I get it. No matter how much money or fame and no matter how many friends a person has, we all face difficult things in life.

But don't forget that these are the things that shape you, if you let them. Because every test you go through is setting you up to be a testimony for God's great name. You can't have a testimony without a test. You've got to go through the stuff, press past the problems, and overcome the adversities to develop your spiritual strength. God will perfect you. He promises. He's able. But you have to lift the weights yourself. You've got to make your spiritual muscles move.

Before making the decision to stay home full-time with our kids and also focus on ministry, my wife, Kanika, was a physical therapist. One of the most important determining factors in a patient's recovery, when it comes to physical therapy, is their willingness to participate in the process. If the PT did all the lifting, no progress would be made. It requires the patient, even if in pain, to push through and cooperate with the therapist to make any forward movement. Similarly, you and I can't just sit back and assume Jesus is going to

You can't have a testimony without a test. You've got to go through the stuff, press past the problems, and overcome the adversities to develop your spiritual strength. God will perfect you. He promises. He's able. But you have to lift the weights yourself. You've got to make your spiritual muscles move.

do all the work for us in our spiritual life. In order to get what God has for us and seize our time right now, we have to put in the work.

Far too many people want a house who don't want to put in the work to make it a home these days. Far too many people want a wedding who don't want to do what is necessary to make it a marriage. Far too many people want a career who don't want to give the effort to make it a calling. But God is saying, "If you want what I have given to you—if you want to have it—you've got to cooperate with Me to perfect My work in you. Stop trying to perfect it on your own. Stop trying to manipulate it into your version of Christian success. Stop pursuing the world's way to gain what I am giving you." God will perfect it in you, but only if you connect with Him so He can do so.

It requires your work. But it also requires your participation with God. What do you think would happen if a patient in physical therapy told the therapist, "You don't need to come to my therapy sessions; I'm good on my own. I can do it myself." No progress would be made that way either. Growth comes through connection with the one trained to help you grow.

Listen, if you were playing basketball in the 1990s on the Chicago Bulls team, and you found yourself down to the wire with time for only one more shot in the game, what would you do? Who would you pass the ball to? Of course, even if you're not a basketball fan, you know that you would pass the ball to Michael Jordan. There is no better player to give it to. No disrespect to you and your mad skills, but you've got to give the ball over to Jordan. That is, if you want to win the game. You know why you give it to Jordan? Because you are confident that he will finish the game. You are confident he'll make the shot.

Now, if you are living your life and facing detours or dead ends over and over again on your spiritual trek, I want to ask you an important question. Are you holding on to the ball too long? Or are you passing it to everyone else but the One you should give it to? Paul tells you loud and clear that Jesus will hit the shot every time. There's no question. Paul says he's confident in this. But you need to give Jesus the ball. You need to cooperate with Him on where He's taking you. You need to work with Him in order to guarantee the victory in your life and purpose this side of heaven. Pass the ball and get the win!

You'll notice in Philippians 1:6 that the word "He" is the subject. That means He is the One doing all the work. It is He who began a good work in you who will perfect it. You're not the one to do the work on your own. You are to connect with the One who knows what He is doing. It's in your connecting, your passing of the ball, your participation with His program, that you find your purpose.

That's why Jesus explained our connection to Him using the vine and branches in John 15. If you've read it, you know what I mean. He is the vine and we are the branches. See, branches don't do anything. Vines have all the nutrition, not the branches. Branches simply connect to the vine and that's how they bear fruit. You will bear fruit and reach your time to shine in life that God has for you if you will learn this art of connecting. Passing the ball. Abiding. Cooperating. Looking to. Trusting. Doing what He says to do. You can word it any number of ways, but it all means the same thing.

He who began a good work in you will bring it about. He'll perfect it. Trust Him. Connect to Him. Trust the power He provides. He's got you. Follow His lead. He knows what He's doing and He knows what He's asking you to do. Yours isn't His first life to perfect. If you haven't noticed, He's been doing this for centuries. And, last I checked, He does what He does really well. Be confident that you will finish, and that you will win. Because this is what you have been saved to accomplish. Walk forward with your head up. Let your heart be strong. Do all that you do with . . . *CONFIDENCE.*

## Scan to Continue

# CHAPTER 7

#

**Pause.** Stop. Hold on. Check yourself. Chill. We know these words. We know all of them very well by now. Mostly we know them because we've experienced them. All the world has experienced these terms, especially during the COVID-19 lockdown of 2020.

These words mean something different to everyone right now, after having lived them for so long. The year 2020 redefined these terms for us because we all felt them as we had never envisioned them before. I know I did. I experienced the whole gamut—from disappointment to understanding.

At first, the lockdown had me feeling down, knowing there were a lot of things I wanted to do that I couldn't do. There were places I had planned on going that I wouldn't be able to go. There were worship services that I was used to having that I wouldn't be able to attend. There was money that needed to be made that wouldn't be made due to the circumstances surrounding us. There were also gatherings with family and friends that I was used to enjoying on a regular basis that suddenly came to a screeching halt.

As the COVID-19 lockdown commenced, I had all of these thoughts running through my mind about the various things I was losing, or missing out on, because everything had shut down.

However, I decided to tap back into my football playing days to see what lessons I could pull from the past to use in this new season of life. I remembered that there are times as a player when things shut down around you. It's usually when you are injured and have to go into rehab. My friend Dak Prescott, quarterback for the Cowboys, knows this all too well. If you saw the play where he suffered his excruciating ankle injury, then you probably saw that realization written all over his face as they carted him off the field, tears streaming. Due to one moment in time, all stopped. Everything changed. And a new focus began: healing and growth.

Players often call this a cocoon season. It's a time to regroup and reset. See, when a caterpillar goes into a cocoon, it's because there's a transformation that needs to take place. There's a lot of isolation and a lot of pain, but there is also an opportunity for greater growth.

Similarly, when things spin out of our personal control—as in the lockdown that started in 2020, we may feel bad about it, but we also need to look for what can be during those times.

As a player in a cocoon season, you get more time to study the playbook. You get more time to ask your coaches questions. You are able to watch more game film so you can figure out what your opponent is really up to. Cocoon season gives a greater currency than playing at times, and that currency is *time*. In the cocoon, you have time you didn't have when you were on the field or in the grind. You now have reallocated time to assess things about yourself and the players around you. Being in the cocoon hurts, but it also grants you the time to level up. It's not the time to sit, sulk, and sour. It's time to prepare yourself for your breakout moment.

A lot of us started to realize this as the COVID-19 lockdown extended from fifteen days to many months. We trusted that if we were willing to cooperate with the lockdown, we could tame the rage of the invisible enemy. I was willing to have my face covered with a mask because even in the lockdown and limitations, that is where safety was said to be found. The lockdown gave me an opportunity to both rest and reset because I was stopped in my tracks from chasing the idol called "Busy" in our culture. Because now Busy was forced to pause. Stop. Hold on. Ultimately, I was forced to . . . *Wait*. It gave me the chance to reevaluate what I value most—my family, time with God and in His Word, and my own growth spiritually. All of these things had taken a hit from my earlier chase after Busy. The lockdown showed me there was something better than Busy. It involved learning to be present right where I am.

I think many of us started to learn these lessons and cooperate as a culture because we recognized that there is value and progression even in a lockdown. We experienced resets individually, but also collectively. Sometimes God has to allow us to be stopped in our pursuits so that we can start again. We've gotten so far off track that it requires a reset. We need a time-out. We need a do-over.

What's more, as we continued with the recommended social distancing, face coverings, and lockdowns, we saw that despite the hardships, good could be accomplished. Paul learned this same truth, in a very different situation, but in a situation that also had his life on pause. He was forced into wait mode, and because of it, he saw God work while he waited well.

We saw in the last chapter that Paul wanted to remind us why we all are here. He wanted to reassure us that when we align our hearts and minds with Christ, He is the one to bring about the destiny and purpose we seek. He takes it upon himself to finish the work He started in us. We also saw that the work He started is a testament to His good work on the cross, which freed us from the eternal bondage and temporal trappings of sin. But Paul doesn't simply say it, as we see in Scripture. He lives what he preaches. If we go over to the letter he wrote to the church at a town called Philippi, we get a glimpse into Paul putting flesh on what he preaches.

In this letter, Paul tells the people who live in Philippi that there is something he wants them to know. He wants them to understand that his circumstances, as difficult as they may be, have brought about a greater good. He wants them to see how the challenges and struggles he personally faced have ushered in all that he had hoped they would. We read this in Philippians 1:12: "Now I want you to know, brethren, that my circumstances have turned out for the greater progress of the gospel."

Paul's circumstances brought about the greater progress of the Gospel. Did you get that? Let me have Paul say it backwards and maybe it will help you grasp what our brother is trying to say: "The gospel's progress is greater, as it turns out, due to my circumstances." In this, Paul is pointing out an important principle for each of us who want to fully experience all that God has for us.

He's letting us know that his circumstances were not for nothing. He is comforting us with his own comfort in saying that the things he had gone through, and what he was still going through at the time of the statement, were not random. They were not by chance. No, what Paul wants us to know is that what happened to him in experiencing a difficult season was intentional and used by God for good. His misery was meaningful and his circumstances were consequential because they turned out for the greater progress of the Gospel of Jesus Christ. So that we don't miss the point, Paul explains it more fully in the next two verses.

So that my imprisonment in the cause of Christ has become well known throughout the whole praetorian guard and to everyone else, and that most of the brethren, trusting in the Lord because of my imprisonment, have far more courage to speak the word of God without fear.

vv. 13–14

As Paul sat in prison, surrounded by four walls and chained to a situation he had no personal power to fix, he tells us, in my paraphrase, "It's all good." Because while he's on lockdown in the midst of a test and a trial, God is using his situation to further the good news of Christ. He's using Paul's pain to change the eternal positioning of those around him.

Why is this important to all of us today? Because that's how God works. And if we are unaware of God's goals and God's agenda, we will get confused by God's movement in our lives.

Many of you know what it's like to be in a situation that you can't fix. You're chained and locked down in a scenario that you have no control to alter. You couldn't make it any better even if you tried. Your hands are tied. You want to adjust things so they will be better but you're imprisoned as Paul is, just in a different way. It may not be a literal prison, but you are still stuck. You are prevented from doing what you want to do. Instead, you must . . . *Wait.*

We've all been there. I'm not just talking about you. I've been there too. During these times, we would like to manipulate the situation with our own hands but we can't. Your money can't fix it. Your friends can't fix it. Your family can't fix it. Your clout can't fix it. Your charm can't fix it. Not this one. Not this time. It's an emotional, spiritual, or circumstantial lockdown of sorts that no one can fix.

When you find yourself in a situation like this, which we all do from time to time, Paul is talking to you. He's not just writing a letter to a church in a town you've never heard of nor will ever visit. He's writing to you. He's telling you because he wants to be sure you know that as you sit in your prison-of-sorts, as he sits in his actual prison, that this seemingly negative situation can turn out for the greater progress of the greater good. He's telling you because he wants you to know that your scenario is not random—your training and testing will not be for nothing. What you are going through, the troubles you are experiencing, as dark as they may seem, will produce light.

The reason Paul wants you and me to know this is because if we don't understand it and cooperate with the program at hand, our pain will become a bit more painful. If we fail to grasp this, then our hurt will become a bit more hurtful. If we ignore this truth and sidestep this spiritual reality, then our depression will wind up being a bit more depressing. Why? Because you'll think that what you are going through, experiencing, and struggling with is only about running you into the ground. You won't realize it's about creating something in you and in others. If you continue thinking your circumstances are for nothing, then your situation will have to continue until it accomplishes what it was put there to produce, and it will take longer to do so. That means a longer . . . *Wait.*

Notice the word *greater* that we saw earlier in Philippians 1:12 is hinged between the circumstances and what comes about due to the circumstances—the furthering of the Gospel. If I were to write it as a mathematical equation, I would take the "greater than" symbol and stick it in the middle of the verse. It would look like this:

$$\text{Gospel} > \text{Circumstances}$$

Paul tells us this because he wants to make sure we know that no matter how great our circumstances may be, they will never be as great as what God creates out of them. No matter how difficult your

What you are going through, the troubles you are experiencing, as dark as they may seem, will produce light. If you continue thinking your circumstances are for nothing, then your situation will have to continue until it accomplishes what it was put there to produce, and it will take longer to do so. That means a longer . . . Wait.

challenges may seem, they will never be more than what God wants to produce from them. No matter how long you feel you are waiting, Paul wants you to know something greater is still progressing. God has a goal in mind. He doesn't just toss messy scenarios at you for no reason. Yet because it can be easy to think that sometimes, Paul is trying to make sure it is perfectly clear that you know what you are going through is not for naught.

What God brings you to in your purpose will be greater than anything you experienced in your pain.

Now, I hear you. You probably want to send me a text right now like "Jonathan, you don't understand how dark my darkness is." Or maybe you want to say that I don't understand how depressing your depression is. Or how anxious your anxiety is. Or how low your low is. And I may not. I may not understand all you are going through. But what I do know is that Paul was tied up in prison in terrible conditions and yet he told us, "It's all good." It was all good because God produced something greater than the pain he endured. So one thing's for sure:

If it's not good yet, God is not done yet.

If you don't see the good God is producing yet, buckle up because it ain't over. If you hang in there and trust Him to do what He does, you will see it. But if you bail, you'll get both the pain and the purposelessness that comes from living outside of God's will. This is a world founded on free will. You *get* to choose. But that also means you have to live with the *consequences* of your choices.

As we discussed in a previous chapter, God works all things out for good to those who love Him and are called according to His purpose (Romans 8:28). You shouldn't be surprised by what you are going through when things get tough and hard times hit because we also saw that Jesus said in John 16:33 (NIV), "In this world, you will have trouble." He didn't say, "In this world, you *might* have trouble." Jesus said you and I *will* have trouble in this world. Bottom line. That's it. But you can still have joy and good cheer when you do because He has overcome the trouble of this world—that same trouble you are going through right now. He's got it. He promises you that what will turn out from the trouble you face will be greater than what you are locked in. It will be worth the struggle once you realize what God has produced because of it.

The reason I'm spending so much time on this truth in these chapters is because I need to make sure you understand this. Too many people miss out on what God has given to them because they don't get this point. Too many people fail to seize their time when it's their turn to rise because they fail to grasp this truth. As a result, they throw in the towel before they ever get to have what God intended for them. But I don't want you to give up. God doesn't want you to quit. Paul has tried to make sure you don't run out of gas in this game called life because the balls that are going to be thrown your way won't be perfect. The hits that are going to come at you are going to hurt. You'll find yourself with bumps and bruises on this journey. But if you choose to stick with it and finish the course, you'll see what God can produce from it. And it will be for the greater good.

My dad used to take me to downtown Dallas when I was a kid, and we would walk the streets. Any time we passed a construction site that had been taped off, my dad would walk with me over to the tape and ask me to look down at what they were digging. "How deep is that, son?" he'd ask.

I'd reply, "It's real deep, Dad."

"You know what that means?" he'd ask.

God allows the situations in your life to be deep so He can take you high. When He wants to do a great work in someone, and that someone is you, you better hold on to your hat. Because if a skyscraper is going to be eighty stories high, it'll need a foundation that can support it.

I knew the answer, but I'd shrug my shoulders to get to hear him tell me why, again.

"It means they plan to build up real high. I know this because the foundation has to be worthy of what is going to be built on top of it."

I'd heard him tell me that before, but I didn't mind each time he said it because there's something profound about words coming out of Tony Evans' mouth that makes you go, "Wow, you're right!"— even if you've heard it before. You know what I'm saying! But what he said was true. If the building was going to be high, the foundation needed to go deep.

A lot of people want a skyscraper life but on a chicken-coop foundation. They don't want to do the work of digging deep spiritually, emotionally, and circumstantially. They just want to lay down a few boards or pour one bag of concrete and call it a day. But skyscrapers don't work that way. And neither does God.

God allows the situations in your life to be deep so He can take you high. When He wants to do a great work in someone, and that someone happens to be you, you better hold on to your hat. You better buckle your seatbelt. You better hang on for the ride, because if a skyscraper is going to be eighty stories high, it'll need a foundation that can support it. Trust me, it's worth the . . . *Wait*.

If junk has happened to you, or is happening to you, just know you are on your pathway to purpose. Be aware that if mess is all around you, you just might be in the process of digging the depth of the hole into which God is about to pour His foundation for you to soar. Paul tells us this from prison because he's gearing our mindsets to understand that what turns out will be much greater than what you're locked in right now.

Some of you reading this know my NFL story. You at least know I got signed by the Dallas Cowboys, because I stated that in the first chapter. But you also know I got cut my first year and wound up sitting out the entire season on my couch. But despite having a bad start, I didn't give up on my dream. I decided to continue putting in the work, and I got called back up again the following year. I wound up playing in the NFL for five years. But, if I were to be honest, I look back on that time and really don't feel like I played in the NFL at all, but rather that the NFL played me. My time there was a whirlwind of disappointment and dashed dreams.

Throughout my career, everything that *could* go wrong, *did* go wrong. And by *everything*, I mean being traded, being cut, even being booed off the field when playing an away game against the New England Patriots at Gillette Stadium. My ankle had been injured on a play and as I was being carted off the field, the Patriots fans were booing and literally throwing cans at me, yelling things like "You suck!" I can tell you one thing for sure about my time in the league—it was tumultuous. Six teams in five years will give you a summary word like that. I only had one big yet simple dream—I wanted to run out of the tunnel for a regular season NFL game with my team. I had many times when I got very close to that dream, but it always seemed to fall short.

The whole time I was going through this apparent failure in my life, I was asking God, *Why? Why are You doing me like this, God? I'm out here trying to lead the players in Bible studies before the games. I'm trying to be a witness for You, and You're sending me all over the place!* I felt like He was punishing me. God knew this was the dream I had always wanted. He knew this was my thing. But despite how much I desired it, nothing was working out for me.

Eventually, in 2009 I decided to retire from a career that never really came to fruition. As I did, I was still thinking, *Why?* I didn't even know what I was supposed to do at that point. I knew what

God was doing with my dad—he's a preacher. I knew what God was doing with my sister Chrystal—she's called to serve her husband and homeschool her five children full time. I knew what God was doing with my sister Priscilla—she's a speaker and author. I knew what God was doing with my brother, Anthony—he's a singer, worship leader, and producer extraordinaire. I knew that everybody in my family was getting what God had for them—everybody but me. I was almost thirty years old by that time and saw myself as the family failure. I tried. Man, I tried hard. Football is no joke. But things just didn't work out.

Yet just two years after I retired, I got a call from the Cowboys. They were calling me to come back! The original team that had signed me out of college was calling my name. You better believe I went back!

I'll never forget the experience of my first game. We were playing against the Jets. I was standing in the tunnel before the game. I was finally getting the opportunity I had always wanted—to run out of the tunnel with an NFL team. I couldn't help but call the one who had made the most impact on me, my dad, while I had the chance. So, I dialed up my dad in the tunnel and said, "Dad, we're here now! I made it! I made it!" 😄

My dad said, "Amen, son. Amen."

But let's pause for a second. Because if you know anything about football, you might be wondering why I had my cell phone in the tunnel right before running onto the field. Players aren't allowed to take their phones with them to the field. That's against the rules. And if that thought crossed your mind, you are exactly right.

The reason I had my cell phone in the tunnel before the game was because I wasn't a player. I was now the team chaplain. They didn't call me back to play, they called me back to pray! I've served in this role for close to a decade now and I've been running out of the tunnel ever since.

As I stood there that day, I realized something. God was saying, "Jon Jon, this was My plan from the very beginning. I knew that your greatest misery would become your greatest ministry. I needed you to experience all the hardships of your journey because like I said in Philippians 1:12, I know that your 'circumstances have turned out for the greater progress of the gospel.' You were saddened by being injured, getting cut, and being sent to other teams, but you have to understand that I had a purpose in mind all along. The people you met. The things you learned. The dynamics you witnessed. The way you grew spiritually. The emotions you experienced. You are now fully prepared to relate to the players in every aspect of their unique lives. This includes your ability to minister to their struggles after enduring your own., See Jon Jon, all of these ingredients were put into the pot to stir up your purpose. I made you who you are today. I equipped you to carry out your role as chaplain on America's Team with both authenticity and depth. I knew my plan was great, that's why I made you . . . *Wait.*"

I finally got it. I now understood. The location of the Gospel on the field of life was much more important than the location of myself in connection with my personal dreams. The same is true in football. When a player gets knocked down on a play but notices that a player on his team still gets the ball across the goal line, the player who was knocked down doesn't stay down and sulk. He doesn't walk off and pout. He doesn't go and complain because he got knocked down. No, he pulls himself up off the ground and celebrates. Why? Because the location of the football is much greater than what happens to him on any individual play.

Paul is sitting in his cell writing Philippians 1:12 to remind you to never think too small. Don't sit in your personal cell in sadness. Paul is cutting a window in the side of your cell to help you see out a bit further than where you are now. You may be concerned about what you are going through or where you are in life. But God is not hating on you. He doesn't have it out for you. He's trying to prepare you for the great things He has for you up ahead. God is always looking at the location of His football. He didn't send His Son, Jesus, to die on the cross just so you could go and do your own thing. Rather, what Christ accomplished is greater than what you may be currently experiencing.

Paul stated it as plainly as anyone could in verse 13, which we looked at earlier. It's worth reading again: "So that my imprisonment in the cause of Christ has become well known throughout the whole praetorian guard and to everyone else." Paul is in jail telling us that his imprisonment has become well known to many people. His imprisonment is not private. He's telling us that it's become public. What's more, in his imprisonment becoming public, many others who talk about Christ have gained a greater courage to do so.

See, Paul wasn't in jail for doing something wrong. He was in jail for a cause bigger than himself. He had been imprisoned for doing something good. Something bad had come his way due to him doing something good. And in life, that happens. It might not be a literal prison, but difficulties can happen when you pursue a good cause.

This reminds me of Martin Luther King Jr. who was in the Birmingham jail in 1963. He was imprisoned for doing something good—for seeking the welfare and rights of black Americans nationwide. John Lewis is another strong example, who from 1960 to 1966 wound up in prison forty times for acting on the belief that everyone deserved equal treatment and equal access in our land. In fact, Lewis often referred to these situations as "good trouble." He was in jail for doing something good.

It also reminds me of the North Carolina student sit-ins. Young students, many of them teenagers, wound up in jail for taking a stand, or actually a seat, in whites-only restaurants where they weren't welcomed. They landed in jail for fighting for justice. In jail for doing good. These and other examples of people being imprisoned for the cause of justice would go on to become well known throughout our culture. As a result, it gave so many more people the courage to advance the ball of justice. And because more people stood up, society had to change. That's how it works.

That's why Paul wasn't complaining in his prison. He was praising God because he knew how God operates. He knew what was more important than his personal comfort. There were people who needed the Gospel, and Paul was doing his part to get the message to them.

That's why you can't throw in the towel when life gets tough. I know so many people who struggled during the earlier months of the COVID-19 lockdown. There were struggles with depression. Struggles with suicidal thoughts. Fear caused so many people to want to give up.

Dak, whom I mentioned earlier, is one guy I'm really proud of. This is because he had the courage to talk openly about his mental health during one of the hardest seasons of his life. As if the emotional weight of the lockdown wasn't enough, he also experienced the unexpected loss of his older brother. His best friend. But he didn't hide his depression or his struggle. Rather than put on a smile and pretend everything was alright, Dak shared with the world what he was going through.

His willingness to speak out as he did brought criticism. Maybe you saw it. Maybe you scratched your head like I did when Skip

Bayless criticized Dak for telling the world he became depressed shortly after his brother passed away. The criticism from Skip took Dak's story to a whole new level. As his story trended, more eyes saw Dak's story and more hearts realized that depression can be walked through.

Millions of people who were struggling, who were sitting in their own dark rooms at the edge of the cliff, saw one of their favorite QBs—their hero—saying he knew right where they sat. He understood those feelings of despair. He admitted they are hard. But he also knew that a person can push through to a stronger tomorrow if they don't throw in the towel and give up.

Dak's personal imprisonment set so many other people free. Similarly, Paul's physical imprisonment brought eternal freedom to a greater portion of the known world. The progress of the Gospel was greater than the prison Paul had been locked in. The progress of God's kingdom is also greater than any difficulties you could ever face. Remember that truth. It'll keep you on life's treadmill when you want to step off. Hang in there. There's always a greater glory on the other side of pain. Don't quit, there is something great right around the corner if you are only willing to . . . *Wait*!!

# CHAPTER 8

# YES

**It's a word to affirm a question.** It can be used to agree with a point. Or it emphasizes something you are about to say. The word *yes* can be used a lot of ways. When Paul used it in prison, he used it to let us all know that what he was about to say wasn't just off the cuff. He thought this through. He knew what he was going to say. And he wanted to shoot down any potential question from the start. Questions like,

"Really?"

"Are you serious?"

"You must be joking. Are you telling the truth?"

Paul knew that what he was about to say from prison would catch everyone by surprise, so he started it out with an affirming word. An emphasizing term. He began by saying, "Yes." What follows ought to surprise all of us.

Now, you may have read this verse before, but just because you have, I don't want you to glance over it this time. Not today. It's too important. This is what Paul said: "Yes, and I will rejoice" (Philippians 1:18).

Paul says it as if someone is in the room talking to him. He's explaining what he's choosing to do, and rather than pause for their objections, he shoots them down from the start. His words before this statement go like this: "What then? Only that in every way, whether in pretense or in truth, Christ is proclaimed; and in this I rejoice" (v. 18). Anticipating the hearer's confusion or pushback on what he had just said, Paul followed it up with

Yes, and I will rejoice.

Yes, I've made my decision. Yes, I know what I'm doing. Yes, I'm in my right mind. Yes, I am able to do this. Yes, this is an option on the table. Yes, I will have joy even when I am in jail.

I don't know about you, but when I sat on that statement and let it soak in, I realized how much I needed to hear those five words from Paul. Maybe you did too.

As I've mentioned, the previous two years before writing this book were the toughest I've ever had to face. I won't go over all the details because I've shared them elsewhere, but ultimately, through the loss and suffering I experienced, alongside my family, I basically found myself in an emotional and spiritual prison. I found myself struggling with a number of things that I just didn't know how to shake or get through.

It was during this time that I ran across these five words Paul had placed between Philippians 1:18 and Philippians 1:19. It's almost like an add-on between major thoughts. It's an emphasis. He wants us to realize, as the reader, that what he is saying has been thought through. These aren't just spiritual-sounding words to send to someone in their time of need. These are his words. His choice. His way of facing his pain.

*Yes*, and I will rejoice.

The reason these five words encouraged me so much is because I knew that Paul was in jail when he stated it. This wasn't a social media post from a beach somewhere telling everyone to keep their chin up in tough times. Paul wasn't placating regarding pain's grip on people's hearts. He understood it because he was in the midst of it himself.

But as I read those five words and began to try to apply them in my own life situation, I started asking internal questions too. I started wondering how in the world Paul was going to praise God in prison. I wondered how in the world Paul was able to still have joy while in jail. The questions continued, but each one was met with a quick reply because evidently Paul had made the decision by choice and not by circumstances. He had made a decision of his *will*.

Yes, and I *will* rejoice.

In other words, Paul was telling himself what he was going to do. Even though he didn't feel like doing it, he was making a decision of the will to do it. This was not a decision of his feelings. He decided to *will* himself to rejoice.

Most people only rejoice and give God praise when they feel like it. They only rejoice and give God praise when they feel He deserves it. They only rejoice and give God praise when the check arrives, the contract is signed, the promotion comes in, the relationship gets good, the diet works, the new car hums, their post gets a lot of likes—and so on and so on. Most people are conditional about when they rejoice and even more conditional when it comes to praising God.

But that's not what Paul is about. Paul is in jail. Paul is locked up. Paul is behind bars. Paul is hungry. Paul is dirty. Paul is uncomfortable and most likely he's also sleep-deprived. That's why his ability to rejoice comes tied to his will. It's a decision. He chooses to rejoice in spite of the circumstances he is in.

One of the reasons this reality of Paul and his leadership was so healing for me, and the reason it can also be healing for you, is because Paul was actually doing the opposite of what you think he would do in the situation he faced. He was turning the tables rather than allowing himself to be defined by the scenario in which he found himself. I can hear Paul saying, "I may be in prison, but I ain't nobody's prisoner."

Paul reminded us all in those five words that what happens to us in life may be out of our control but how we respond to it is always within our control. Nobody gets to make that decision for you but you. A lot of people don't know how necessary this truth is to understand and apply, which limits them in living out the full expression of their time to shine. A lot of people crumble beneath the weight of their emotions, which prevents them from pursuing their passions and purpose wholeheartedly. But Paul has given us a prescription for how to spiritually medicate our souls so that we don't wind up short of the goal line of our life's calling.

When discussing mental health at this time in our culture, a common part of the discussion revolves around medications. Psychiatrists prescribe medications when they are trying to counterbalance what the patient is experiencing emotionally and chemically within. They want to take the edge off of what the person is going through by seeking to even out their emotions. And while sometimes medication is helpful—I don't want to pretend that it's not—what Paul is telling us in this passage is that there is also a spiritual pill. He has a spiritual approach to get you out of the dungeon. He has a spiritual secret to break you free from solitary confinement. His secret is summed up in five words. I'm sure you know them by now:

Yes, and I will rejoice.

In other words, rejoicing is a decision you make even when you don't feel like it because it adds tension to counterbalance your trials. It adds tension to soften the strain of tribulations, to reduce the pain from the pull of the test. It's a bungy cord strapped to you in your dungeon so that you can be pulled back to the reality of how good God is even when things don't seem very good at all.

When you choose to rejoice, you are declaring that even though you may have circumstances to contend with in life, the circumstances will not have you. The circumstances will not dictate your emotional dignity. The circumstances will not overpower you. This is a critical life principle that the Bible states many times:

I will bless the LORD at all times; His praise shall continually be in my mouth.

Psalm 34:1

Rejoice in the Lord always; again I will say, rejoice!

Philippians 4:4

Rejoice always; pray without ceasing; in everything give thanks; for this is God's will for you in Christ Jesus.

1 Thessalonians 5:16–18

Notice in the last verse that it doesn't say to give thanks *for* everything. It says to give thanks *in* everything. So even though you may be in difficult circumstances, a thanksgiving ought to be *in* you. When you can grasp that and choose to rejoice, you'll discover that God has given you a counterweight for your emotions. He has given you a spiritual prescription through the difficult times in life you are experiencing now, have experienced in the past, or will experience in the future.

One of the positions that I love to watch the most in football is the cornerback because in my opinion, the cornerbacks are the most athletic guys on the field. The reason is due to the fact that they have to essentially guard someone while simultaneously having no idea where that someone is going. Cornerbacks have to backpedal when their opponent is running forward. They have to run sideways when the person they're covering is running ahead. They have to constantly be observing, assessing, adjusting, moving, chasing. It's a masterpiece to see.

If I played cornerback, my name would be toast because I would be nowhere around the receiver I had been assigned to guard. I honestly have no idea how these corners can stay with a guy, not knowing where he's going. It seems like a disadvantage to me, and truth be told, many times it is. That's why coaches will often tell their cornerbacks that they need to have a short-term memory.

Now, this doesn't mean that you don't remember the mistake you made on the last play, but it does mean that the cornerback needs to let go of the past and *will* himself into conquering the next play. Because if he doesn't operate with a short-term memory, by holding on to the fact that he just got beat on the last play, he'll continue to get beat. He'll continue to fall short. And any time a player continues to get beat, it starts a cycle that typically plants his butt on the bench. Sit on a bench too long and you get sent home. Things will continue to spiral downhill and out of control. Why? Because the

Even though you may be in difficult circumstances, a thanksgiving ought to be in you. When you can grasp that and choose to rejoice, you'll discover that God has given you a counterweight for your emotions. He has given you a spiritual prescription through the difficult times in life.

player who just got beat allowed getting beat to beat up on him. If and when a person allows this, the beatdown just goes on.

A lot of people don't understand what Paul is saying when he refuses to give in to the pressures of the pain around him. He's saying that he's going to *will* himself to the next play. He's going to *will* himself to trust God. He's going to *will* himself to believe that, while things might be a mess up until now, anything is fair game. Things can change. Paul is saying to himself, "Can I be a beast on the next play? . . . *Yes!*"

## Joy vs. Happiness

Before we go any further on this, I want to point out that Paul is telling us he rejoiced. He never said he was happy in prison. He never said he was delighted in the dungeon. What he said was that he chose to have joy in jail. There's a difference between happiness and joy. A big difference. Most people in American culture will tell you that they want to be happy. I hear people telling me that all of the time when I'm counseling them or giving them advice. They're like, "Hey J, I just want to be happy."

I smile in response but think to myself, *Good luck with that!* Because I already know where that story goes. If someone is chasing after happiness, then they are chasing something that was made to avoid them. They are seeking that which was designed to elude them. See, *happiness* is totally contingent upon what is *happening.* And because you and I can't control everything that is happening, we cannot catch, hold on to, secure, or maintain happiness. To chase happiness is to chase something that was made to get away from you. It ebbs and flows as the circumstances ebb and flow. Nobody's circumstances will ever be one hundred percent happiness-worthy.

Why? Because we are sinners living in a sinful world inhabited by other sinners.

That's why so many people today are so tired. They're tired because they are on a constant sprint after happiness. Yet happiness, even when you do catch it, is fleeting. The referee blows his whistle as soon as you make the grab. The play is over. Start again. See, Paul is not telling us that he is happy. He's not telling us to chase after being happy. He's telling us that he is choosing to rejoice, no matter what comes around.

So, if happiness is based on what is happening, what, then, is joy? Joy is based on an internal faith. Joy involves trusting God no matter what happens. Joy means believing what God has told you will come about. Joy involves a heartfelt belief that God's Word is true. No matter what the circumstances feel like outside, you can rejoice by simply deciding you're going to believe God and His good plans for you. You can be stable when you choose to rejoice because even if the winds and waves crash down on you, you are connected to the solid Rock of Jesus Christ.

In order to progress in this thing called life and *get what God has given you*, you must realize how powerful it is to have a strong faith, especially when you're in weak circumstances. You must never allow your prison to determine your praise. You must never allow your challenges to determine your choices. You must never allow your weaknesses to determine your willingness. And you must certainly never allow your feelings to determine your function.

Because when you do, all chaos will erupt around you, as you have now given a foothold to the enemy. You have given an open door to the opposition. And trust me, the opposition is ready to rush through that door at any given moment—all he needs is a small crack. You must master your mind if you are going to maximize your mission in this life. Your mind must align underneath God's Word. Your heart must adjust to God's rule. Your emotions must be leashed by the truth so that your emotions are following the truth and not the other way around.

Yes, I understand. I get it. You may feel like you are in prison. Whether it's an emotional, financial, relational, circumstantial, or even a pandemic-based prison, I hear you. I've been there. I'm no different than you. But you can be in a prison and not be a prisoner. That decision is up to you. Paul leashed his feelings so that they followed his function. And if we can get more people to do what Paul did, what Paul taught—what he modeled for all of us—we would have more people reaching the end zone of this life and saying as he did, "I have fought the good fight, I have finished the course, I have kept the faith" (2 Timothy 4:7).

## Focus on Where You Are Headed

Paul fought the good fight by keeping the faith. We witness how this faith impacted him because right after he tells us he is going to rejoice in prison, he explains why. First Paul said,

Yes, and I will rejoice,

then he followed it up with the all-important why:

for I know that this will turn out for my deliverance.

Paul's rejoicing hinged on his faith. "For I know" reflects faith. He shows us his faith right there in jail. Once he realizes that God will bring about a deliverance from this situation for His glory and the

You must master your mind

if you are going to maximize

your mission in this life. Your

mind must align underneath

God's Word. Your heart must

adjust to God's rule. Your

emotions must be leashed by

the truth so that your emotions

are following the truth and not

the other way around.

furtherance of the Gospel, Paul decides to *will* himself to the next play. God hasn't yet delivered him when he chooses to rejoice. He's still in prison. But he knows—he has faith—that God will deliver him. And because of that, he chooses to rejoice right where he is. He chooses to say . . . *Yes*.

My wife and I decided to homeschool our kids when the COVID-19 pandemic hit our country. Since my wife was at home full-time already, she took on the majority of the work. Keep in mind, we have five kids under the age of eleven as I'm writing this book. It's chaos! We're in the middle of the woods with no navigation tools.

So while Kanika handles the bulk of the teaching, I get to do the fun stuff. The field trips. I get to teach the real-life things. Sometimes I drive them around neighborhoods and we talk about real estate. Or I'll drive them around businesses and talk to them about business and economics. And when we're not driving, I'll discuss things with them that they probably would never learn in school—things like paying bills, investing, taking risks. I show them how to write a check to pay for the electricity we all use. I've taken it as my role and responsibility to teach my kids these all-important things because, at the end of the day, these are the things that we all face in the "real world."

One of the field trips we recently planned was to a garden. One of our friends has a pretty big garden, so I took the kids over to check it out. I wanted them to see the plants, the soil, and what it takes for food to grow. My son J2 wasn't feeling it. He wasn't excited about this field trip. He was like, "Gardening? C'mon Dad! That's a terrible idea for a field trip! I'd rather play basketball! Or better yet, we can go home, and you can take me on a field trip upstairs so I can play Fortnite!"

I said, "J2, if there is a food shortage in America, we're going to have a problem. We all need to learn how to grow our own food.

Also, you've been asking me how people in the Bible lived so long and some of the reason why is because they didn't eat fast food. They ate slow food. They had to wait for it to come out of the ground. Then they prepared it, cooked it, and ate it."

J2's eyes glazed over like two doughnut holes. He was hearing me, but he had checked out from actually listening. So we kept walking around the garden. But as we kept walking, J2 started to complain even more. He was throwing his head back. He was grumbling about how hot it was. He was letting everyone know that he didn't want to be there at all, let alone learn about a garden.

That's when my friend Kelli, the owner of the garden, tried to encourage him to get involved by handing him some shears and asking him to cut some okra from the okra plant. J2 looked at her like she had asked him to take the stairs all the way to the top of the Empire State Building. Yet, when he saw the boy-you-better-do-what-Kelli-says-right-now-or-I'm-gonna-take-care-of-you-when-I-get-home look on my face, he reluctantly turned and started cutting the okra. He then carelessly threw the harvested okra into the gardening pail like it was garbage, continuing to let us all know that he felt imprisoned by this field trip.

As you can imagine, I had had enough by then. So, I took him to the side and said, "J2, listen. With the way you're acting, you're not going to be able to go swimming in Kim and Kelli's pool. I brought everyone's swimsuits, but it looks like you're gonna have to sit this one out because of your attitude."

J2's eyes opened as wide as saucers. "Pool?" he asked. "You didn't tell me there was a pool."

"I shouldn't have to tell you there's a pool, J2," I replied. "I need you to act right regardless. But, yes, there's a pool." I then opened up the gate so he could see the pool for himself. After which he started running around the garden, tossing his head back in laughter and yelling out, "Oooooh, yeah, baby!" All of a sudden, he was cheerfully cutting okra and tossing them into the pail like he was taking shots in a basketball game. He was having fun. He was dancing. He was making up songs. He obviously had a new perspective of the garden!

I called to him, "J2, how are you dancing in the garden now when you were just miserable a minute ago?"

He said, "It's simple. You told me that next up is the pool!"

J2 could now dance in his place of misery because his focus changed to what his Daddy showed him. All of us need to understand what J2 was saying. He was saying that now that he understood where his father was taking him, he could rejoice in the situation he was in.

Yes, he might be hot. Yes, he might be sweaty. But in just a bit there would be a pool with fresh water to cool him down. And as we saw in the last chapter, God has a good plan for you. In His Word, He has given you a glimpse as to where you are going. He who began a good work in you will complete it. So, when you know that, you can dance in the heat. Run in the garden. Work with joy. Why? Because you have faith in where you are going.

Paul is letting us know that even when things get tough and times get trying, God has a purpose for the pain. He has a reason for the sorrow. He has a plan for your life that, if you will just choose to align your emotions and responses under the divine direction of His will, you will get to see come about. The sooner you choose, like Paul, to rejoice, the sooner you will usher in the timing for your divine destiny in life. Will you rejoice right now? I hope your answer is . . . *Yes*!!

# CHAPTER 9

# NOW

**Less than two months after my mom passed away** following a heroic fight against cancer, I was called upon to speak on a stage I never imagined I'd be on. It was the National Religious Broadcasters (NRB) annual convention. I remember attending these conventions as a kid with my dad and watching my sisters and mom hand out cards or cassette tapes about his ministry. I remember seeing the Christian "celebrities" of those days walk by as well. This is where the hustle took place. Where Christian leaders met. The plans and partnerships were made.

You may have seen a video that's gone viral of my dad preaching in a suit at just thirty-seven years old on the NRB convention stage. This is where he got his start preaching on a national scale. This is where people heard him and said, "Wow, he can preach!" Later, my mom would go on to serve on the board of directors, a role she treasured and handled with loving care. Just imagine going from handing out free cassettes at a convention to serving on its prestigious board of directors. God knows what He's doing. He'll get you there.

So when I got the call that I needed to pinch-hit for one of the speakers who was too sick to come speak at that time—just a week before the event—a lot of these memories flooded me. Memories of attending as a kid. Memories of my dad's historic start. Memories of my mom's faithful service. I was honored by the invitation and of course I accepted the invitation to speak at the opening-night main event kicking off the 2020 conference.

But as I started to prepare what I would preach on, thoughts poured in about the previous year's convention. The previous year we experienced a major high in our family's life. After all the studying, preparing, and preaching my dad had done over the course of his life, he was being inducted into the NRB Hall of Fame. This was a tremendous award for him to receive, not only as a pastor and Bible teacher but also as an African-American. My dad had many firsts as an African-American. He was the first African-American to be accepted into the doctoral program at the prestigious Dallas Theological Seminary. He was the first African-American to have a nationwide Bible-teaching radio show carried on multiple national radio stations. He was the first African-American to write a study Bible and full Bible commentary. And now, he was about to become the first African-American to receive the honor of entry in the NRB Hall of Fame.

In fact, nearly all of our family had flown out to Los Angeles for the ceremony. Both of my parents, both of my sisters, some of their kids, and my brother—we were all there for this historic event in our family's life. As you might suspect, we were extremely excited to be there! We wore smiles all week long.

I hadn't been to an NRB convention since I was a kid, and going that year brought back so many memories. Picking up my badge for the week gave me that familiar feeling of belonging to something bigger than myself—something good, something for God.

My dad is my hero, so I couldn't have been more excited about this moment for him. For the family. For the life of the ministry, The Urban

Alternative. For all of it. My siblings and I were just grinning from ear to ear all week. But, despite all of our enthusiasm, my dad could barely smile at all. Priscilla and I noticed it first. We were confused. So we would nudge him at a meal or when walking the halls and ask, "Daddy, aren't you excited? You ready?" To which he'd just nod his head.

Not getting the answer we expected, we would add something like "It's a lifetime achievement award, Daddy. We're happy for you. Are you excited to get it?"

To which he would reply, "I'm doing okay."

Sometimes I'd let it drop there. Other times I'd push it because I was confused. "Dad, what's going on?" I'd ask. "You're about to be inducted into the NRB Hall of Fame. This is one of the mountaintops. This isn't a valley. But you've got a grimace on your face. What's really going on? Are you okay?"

He would shrug and say, "Jon Jon, I'll be alright."

We had finally reached the day before the event, and the anticipation was building for all of us. We decided to grab something to eat together—Priscilla, my dad, and me—in between various interviews we were all having at the convention. "Tomorrow's the big day, Daddy," Priscilla said, still trying to lift his spirits to match the occasion. "Tomorrow's your day!"

He just replied, "We'll get there when we get there."

I said, "Dad, what's wrong? Are you okay?"

He said, "We'll talk a little bit later."

Priscilla and I looked at each other with the confusion and concern from our hearts coming through our eyes by then. We didn't understand why he was so somber when we were so thrilled. We didn't get why he was so low when he had made it so high.

Friday finally rolled around, and I knocked on his door. Priscilla was standing there outside the door already, still in her pajamas. Chrystal and Anthony had also started to make their way down to the door. They ran through the hall like kids and we all knocked on his door again. He came to the door, opened it, and let us in. Didn't even say hi. He just walked to the bed to lie back down. We said, "Dad, it's Friday. Today you are going to be inducted into the NRB Hall of Fame."

He said, "I'm doing alright. We'll talk about it later."

"You sure, Dad?" I asked.

"I love you, Jon Jon," he replied, totally avoiding the question.

"I love you too, Dad," I said, completely confused.

The night finally came. We all sat around the table as a family. During the other speakers' times, I looked over and saw my dad taking notes. Filling up his note sheet. The grimace he had all week was even more pronounced. "Dad, you excited? You're up next," I whispered, checking on him.

"I love you, Jon Jon," he whispered to me again, then went back to writing his notes.

"I love you too, Dad," I replied.

Shortly after that, they called his name. They gave him the honor. He went up. Delivered a powerful message. Took pictures, halfway smiling, looking as if he was just trying to get through it. All of my siblings and I kept checking on him because he didn't seem quite right. After the event, we went to the greenroom and asked him again, "Dad, come on now. Tell us what's going on. We're here at NRB. You're always excited here. You love it here. Now, you just got inducted into the Hall of Fame with a grimace on your face. Can you please tell us what's going on?"

"Meet me in my room in ten minutes and I'll tell you" was all he had to say.

And man, you talk about all of our hearts beating fast and all of the goose bumps on our arms. We quickly went to his room and knocked on the door. He opened the door and told us to come on in. He sat on his stool and we all sat on the couch. Once we were seated, he said, "Kids, I know this was supposed to be an exciting time, and it is. I am honored that the National Religious Broadcasters Association would seek to honor the work that has been done through The Urban Alternative and everything in ministry that has taken place with me and your mom." He paused. "But tonight, we face the hardest time in our family's history."

As he said that, a chill went up my spine and I looked at him intently, trying to discern what he was about to say. He continued, "We're facing the hardest time."

I asked, "Why, Dad?"

He said, "Because your mom has just been diagnosed with a terminal form of cancer that the doctors have no answer for. She's in stage 4. It has come all the way across her abdomen. There is nothing that we are able to do. I've talked to the best doctors. I went high and I went low. I went everything in between, but there is absolutely nothing they can do about it. So if I've been somber all week, it's because we're facing the hardest time we've ever faced in our family."

About a minute of silence took place as we sat there in shock, trying to digest what we were facing as a family in that moment. It seemed like this news took away all of the achievements and celebration. It seemed like this news wiped away everything that had happened up until that point. All of the joy was just gone, like a deflated balloon. That moment was both terrifying and devastating.

Wailing broke the silence as we were all shaken back into the reality of the moment and saw our dad across the room, crying. He had gotten up and could no longer contain himself. Priscilla and Anthony ran over to him to comfort him. I just sat there, stoic. I was trying to digest all of the information I had just heard, to process it. My brother-in-law was also there and he turned his back and started to cry.

At the height of what seemed like it should be a season of celebrating, we were gathered as a family absolutely devastated. We had just heard the hardest news we had ever heard in our family's history. We didn't know how to take it. We felt beaten. We felt bruised. Yet as all of this crying took place, I remembered my mom. I thought, "Oh, my mom is sitting here. Let me see how she's doing." She had sat through it all, comfortable and stoic.

"Mom, are you doing okay?" I asked.

She replied to all of us. "Everyone come here and sit down." So we did. She had given us some time to process the news and process the devastation that had hit us in that moment. But then she said, "I have something to say."

My mom went on to share her heart with us. She said, "You do know what this is, don't you? It's called spiritual warfare. You do know that we have had six deaths in the last two years in our family and that the enemy has been attacking us. Something has been coming up against our family."

Her question hit us hard. We listened intently. She continued, "We must be doing something right because the enemy is taking notice. God is allowing these things to happen. He is allowing these things to be shaken up. And when we face spiritual warfare, or when we face things that come against our family, the Evans family will not tuck our tails and run. We prepare to attack."

I looked at my sister, and she looked at me. My mom went on, "I understand that you are sad. I understand that this is a hard time. I understand that you had a different expectation. I understand that this wasn't what you were expecting to hear. I understand that this hurts. But you need to understand what this is so that you can assume the posture that you need to have, moving forward. We will not tuck our tails and run. You will get ready to attack."

We let my mom's words sink in, deep into our hearts as she went on, "If you are called to preach, you will preach. If you are called to write, you will write. If you are called to proclaim, you will proclaim. If you are called to lead a Bible study, you will lead it."

We sat there, hanging on every word. "Now, I have every expectation that you will love me, care for me, pray for me, and be there for me," she continued. "I have every expectation that you will do that as my family. But God has an expectation too. And that is that you always remember, through thick and thin, that you are here to serve the purposes of God."

I said, "Mom, how can you be talking about ministry at a time like this?"

She said, "Because that's why you're here, son. That's why you're here. It's the reason why you exist. What do you mean—how can I be talking about ministry at a time like this? Son, that's why you're here. And everything—including pain and anguish—even that which seems counterintuitive, even that which you didn't expect, or the opposition that comes up against you—it's all a distraction. It's designed to distract you from the reason why you are here. So you will stand up, hold your head up, and be strong. You will continue to do the work of the ministry."

I'm telling you what my mom told me that night because as you are on your journey and as you set out to embrace this truth that your time is now to get what God has given you, I want to remind you that you will face opposition. You will go through something that is difficult. You will face lows in life. But no matter what you face, whether it's in your family, your ministry, your emotions, your finances, your relationships, your health—whatever it is—remember:

You are here to serve the purposes of God. That's the time it is right . . . *Now*.

*Now* is your time to serve the purposes of God.

You are too close. The Promised Land is just over the horizon. Do not stop. Do not drop your head. Do not slow down because obstacles are put in your path. God will allow a person to be shaken because He uses that to move them forward.

There are some people reading this book who need to hear this encouragement. There is someone with their eyes fixed on this page who needs this message. Let me remind you, you are not waiting on your time to arrive. Your time is *now*. But Satan will try to convince you otherwise. He will try to distract you.

You live out the purpose of your time right now by pushing through the pains and difficulties in this life. You don't wait for everything to be perfect before you serve God. You serve Him right now, right where you are with what you have at your disposal.

I played in the NFL for a few years, so my illustrations often come from there (or my kids)! And I want to tell you what every player who plays on Sunday is thinking about during the game. They are thinking about Monday. And every college football player who plays on Saturday is thinking about Sunday. And every high school football player who plays on Friday, if you asked them, would tell you they are thinking about Saturday. Why? Because every time a player is playing the game, they are thinking about the next day. The next day is when you have to watch the film and be held accountable for your previous performance.

I remember that when I was playing, if I made a good block, I would be thinking, "Oh yeah, that's going to look good on film tomorrow!" Or if I missed something or didn't do it right, I'd be thinking, "Aaah, I know I'm going to have to watch that mistake tomorrow!"

My mom was letting us know that day as we sat in a hotel room in California that we had better stay focused on what God has called us to do because there would come a day when we would be held accountable for how we played. Just like my coach would do after every football game. He would pull down the screen, turn on the overhead projector, pick up the red pointer, and ask, "Were you out there bearing the image of the uniform that I gave you, based on the playbook I wrote for you in order to execute? Or were you out there doing your own thing? Playing your own game? Don't answer that. Because we're about to watch the film right now."

In 2 Corinthians 5:10, Paul tells us this same thing, "For we must all appear before the judgment seat of Christ, so that each one may be recompensed for his deeds in the body, according to what he has done, whether good or bad." You cannot lose focus, no matter what you face, because your mission is to pursue this thing called life with tomorrow in mind. Your focus must be on Christ, not the crisis. On God, not the grind. On obedience, not the obstacles. Because one day God is going to pull down His cosmic screen, turn on His Holy Ghost overhead projector, and pick up His blood-of-Jesus red pointer. He's going to sit you down and His only concern will be: "Did you serve my purposes? Or did you play by your own schemes? Don't answer that because we're going to watch the film right now."

See, sometimes in life we can get to the place where we're serving our purposes instead of serving the God who made us. We are more concerned about our likes than His love. We do what we can in our own dog and pony show in order to promote our agenda rather than aiming to advance His agenda. But if God gave you this life to live,

Your focus must be on Christ, not the crisis. On God, not the grind. On obedience, not the obstacles. Because one day God is going to sit you down and His only concern will be: "Did you serve my purposes?"

He will certainly also give you all you need to live it to the fullest (John 10:10). If He placed the hope for purpose in your heart, He will also place the path to purpose beneath your feet.

God doesn't always call the qualified. But He always qualifies the called. You don't need to be chasing comments, chasing views, chasing notoriety when God has already commented, viewed, and given notice of His purpose for you. Getting what God has given you is easier than we often make it out to be. It's all about abiding in Him and letting Him work out His goals both in and through you. Align your heart with Christ's and He will reveal to you His will, His plan, His purpose for your life right . . . *Now*.

Growing up, I had a toy poodle named Solomon. The only reason we had a toy poodle was because that's what my two older sisters wanted for our family dog! If it had been me choosing the dog, we would have gotten something a little tougher. But this toy poodle loved to run around in circles, chasing its own tail. I'd get home from school and see this dog running around in circles and I would think, *Does this dog not know that his mouth is on his face and his tail is on his rear end? He wasn't created to catch his own tail. That's just a lot of movement with no progress.*

At twelve years old, I came home to the sound of growling in the back room. There was so much growling going on in the back room that I ran to see what was wrong. When I made it to the room and opened the door, I saw what I didn't think I would ever see. Our dog had caught his own tail! But after a minute of my standing there watching him in shock, he had to let go. He needed to let go because he was too uncomfortable to stay in that position.

Now sure, I imagine he had a moment of dog satisfaction when he eventually caught what he had been chasing for so long. But that's not what he was made for. And he couldn't stay like that!

We have to be careful in our Christian environments and spiritual spheres to not do the same. Because sometimes we can get so involved in what we are doing that we are not actually progressing. We're just running around in circles. We're just running around chasing something that will never satisfy, and that could never last even if we did eventually catch it. We are setting our own target with our own tails. But the tail was never designed to wag the dog. The dog is designed to wag the tail. Oftentimes we've got it backward, which is why we can spend a lifetime chasing after something only to find out, at the end, that it was the wrong something all along.

To get what God has given you, right now, you need to regain your focus. Put your focus where it needs to be—on the Gospel of Jesus Christ and the advancement of His kingdom. Serve the purposes of God. Be a positive impact on your generation, and those to come. Do as Paul did:

> I do not regard myself as having laid hold of it yet; but one thing I do: forgetting what lies behind and reaching forward to what lies ahead, I press on toward the goal for the prize of the upward call of God in Christ Jesus.
>
> Philippians 3:13–14

Press on. Forget the past mistakes. Let go of the past losses. Push through the memories of past miseries. Press on. There is a goal up ahead. There is a prize to pursue. And yes, I know you face opposition in your life. I have faced it in my own life. We all do. Pain does not discriminate. A few years ago, I lost my dear friend and cousin, Wynter Pitts, at the age of thirty-eight. Her heart just stopped. She suddenly passed, with four girls and a husband left behind. Not long after that, my little cousin Michael, who was only twenty-eight years old, lost his wife, who was just thirty. She found out that she had a tumor and passed away the very next day. My grandfather, our Two-Daddy and the original Kingdom Man as we call him, died just a month before my mom. I get it. It's painful. It is hard sometimes. But regardless, we press on.

Whether your loss involves the loss of life, the loss of dreams, the loss of a business, the loss of health, the loss of income, or the loss of relational harmony—whatever it may be—you are to press on. You are to prepare yourself to go on the offensive in this thing called life. You are to do as Galatians 6:9 says to do, "Let us not lose heart in doing good." Other translations say, "Do not grow weary in doing good." Because even though it's hard, even though there is opposition, even though you may never achieve the dreams you had hoped to because they were your dreams, and not God's, you must realign yourself with the goal. What goal? Serving the purposes of God. Why? Because that is how you seize your time and get what God has given you—both for the *now* and for the forever.

December 30, 2019, was the last time I spent time with my mom. But a week before that, she was living between heaven and earth. I knew it. We all knew it. She would say things like "Do you see my mom? She was just sitting over there." We would look over and her mom, who passed away years before, was clearly not sitting there—at least that we could see. Or my mom would ask, "Do you see these colors? They are unbelievable. So beautiful!"

We would smile and respond, "We don't see the colors, Mom, but we know you do."

She would talk like this because she was living somewhere between heaven and earth. But one thing she said stayed with me the most. She said, "The award. The award. They are about to give me my award!"

Even though it's hard, even though there is opposition, even though you may never achieve the dreams you had hoped to because they were your dreams and not God's, you must realign yourself with the goal. What goal? Serving the purposes of God. Why? Because that is how you seize your time and get what God has given you—both for the now and for the forever.

When I heard her say this, I felt peace. I felt peace in the realization of the truth of what she was saying. "Enjoy that award, Mom," I said. "Enjoy it." See, she could enjoy it because she had served the purposes of God. Through thick and thin, she served. Whether receiving no attention or a lot of attention, she served. In times of little money or in times of having enough, she served. In seasons of health and in seasons of sickness, she served the purposes of God. Right through to the finish.

My mom would want me to tell you this right now. If she were here while I was writing this book, I know she would say, "Just remind them, Jon Jon, that there is a reward."

There is a reward for all you do for Christ. Don't lose your focus. Don't tuck your tail and run. Keep pushing. Keep fighting. Keep striving. Keep pursuing. You will get all that is planned for you both in time and in eternity when you choose to serve the purposes of God.

And, as any mother would, my mom would probably nudge me again and say, "Don't forget to tell them this too, Jon Jon: *Now* is as good a time as any to do it."

I would respond and say, "I agree, Mom. I'll tell them straight up."
*YOUR TIME IS NOW!*

**Scan to Finish**

**Get your free copy of the exclusive**
***Your Time Is Now Soundtrack* right NOW!!**

**Scan to Download**

# ACKNOWLEDGMENTS

I want to thank Bethany House Publishers and Baker Publishing Group for their partnership on this timely book and their belief in the need for this message. I want to especially say thank you to Andy McGuire for his initiation of the project, Heather Hair for her collaboration on the writing, and Sharon Hodge in reviewing and interacting with the content. I want to thank the marketing team: Deirdre Close, Stephanie Smith, Holly Maxwell, and Mycah McKeown, and a big thanks goes to Dan Pitts for the cover design. I also want to thank Pharris Photos & Philms for the videos in this book.

# MINISTRY SUMMARY

**JONATHAN EVANS** is a pastor, speaker, mentor, and author who speaks passionately and powerfully about his relationship with God and has a burning desire to share his faith with others. He serves on the pastoral staff at Oak Cliff Bible Fellowship, a nondenominational church in Dallas, Texas, with his pastor, friend, and father, Dr. Tony Evans. Jonathan has roles in both the local church and in the national ministry, The Urban Alternative.

Jonathan has a goal of building a legacy that leaves an impact. A dynamic speaker, he has shared at men's conferences, youth events, churches, and other venues throughout the United States. Jonathan has also written several books, including *Different, Get in the Game: A Spiritual Workout for Athletes* (with Dr. Tony Evans) and *Kingdom Family Devotional* (with Dr. Tony Evans). Jonathan has also created powerful video and audio presentations to accompany his teaching, including spoken word videos that showcase his ability to deliver his messages with energy, creativity, and relevance.

## Chaplain of the Dallas Cowboys and Ministry to Athletes

Jonathan was an NFL fullback for the Dallas Cowboys after playing college football at Baylor University and a season with the Berlin Thunder of the European NFL. During his career he also was on the roster of the San Diego Chargers, Tennessee Titans, Buffalo Bills, Washington Redskins, and Houston Texans. He serves as the chaplain for the Dallas Cowboys, where he uses biblical principles and his own experiences to minister to the needs of today's players. He is available on the sidelines at every game to pray for the team members and to be a voice of encouragement when they need it. Jonathan also counsels the players about issues in their personal lives and offers prayers and devotions at team meetings. With all the stress and pressure involved in professional football, Jonathan sees it as his mission to point the team members toward Jesus Christ.

Jonathan also has a special passion to impact today's young athletes by equipping and encouraging them in their faith. He often uses sports analogies and stories to drive home a consistent and relevant message about commitment, motivation, and faith.

## Generate Nation

Jonathan is the founder of Generate Nation, an outreach of Oak Cliff Bible Fellowship. This ministry, which focuses on young adults, holds weekly Bible studies, monthly special meetings, and major catalytic events, seeking to create an atmosphere of challenging teaching, authentic conversation, and growing relationships. These gatherings are diverse, transparent, and relevant, with a special emphasis on practical teaching about topics such as dating and relationships, forgiveness, living as a single person, trials and tests, roles in marriage, what it means to be a man and woman, and how to live a life of faith in the contemporary world. In addition to solid biblical teaching, Generate offers creative ways for connecting with God's message through music and spoken word poetry.

Jonathan's vision is to nurture spiritually vibrant young adults who crave to be discipled into the character, conduct, and attitude of Christ for the purposes of individual spiritual growth, family health, church service, and community restoration. It is a place where young adults can be known, loved, valued, spiritually developed, and commissioned in their unique giftedness to edify the body and go make disciples.

Generate is "a place for you to believe, belong, and become all that God has purposed for your life." Its innovative style has made it a place for people to find and follow Jesus Christ with passion, authenticity, and commitment.

# NOTES

**Chapter 2: But**

1. As quoted in Calvin Watkins, "'We Weren't Supposed to Win': How the Cowboys Mounted One of the Greatest Comebacks in Team History," *Dallas Morning News*, September 20, 2020, https://www.dallasnews.com/sports/cowboys/2020/09/20/we-werent-supposed-to-win-how-the-cowboys-mounted-one-of-the-greatest-comebacks-in-team-history/.

**Chapter 4: Go**

1. *Merriam-Webster*, s.v. "go (*v.*)," accessed December 28, 2020, https://www.merriam-webster.com/dictionary/go.